Unlocking
Your
Intuition

Unlocking Your Intuition

7 Keys to Awakening Your Psychic Potential

Carol Ann Liaros

4th Dimension Press ■ Virginia Beach ■ Virginia

Contents

Foreword
by Kevin J. Todeschi

As the Executive Director and CEO of Edgar Cayce's Association for Research and Enlightenment, I have had the opportunity to meet a number of very talented professional intuitives who help individuals in a variety of ways by sharing their psychic talents. Carol Ann Liaros is one such individual. For decades her work has gained a tremendous reputation because of her ability to help individuals "where they are at" by giving them insights into every concern in life from health and well-being to relationship issues, from solving financial stress to finding (and living out) their missions in life. In addition to her talents as a psychic counselor and mentor, she is also an incredible teacher and excels at helping individuals to draw upon their own psychic birthright, which is a part of us all.

I have known Carol Ann for more than twenty-five years—first as a professional psychic, conference speaker, and teacher, and later as personal friend and co-author of *Edgar Cayce on Auras and Colors*. She began her psychic work back in the 1960s, first by practicing on her friends, and later as a research subject working with the Human Dimensions Institute at Rosary Hill College. She became known for her accuracy and her conviction that everyone could be trained to use and experience his or her own psychic perception.

That conviction eventually led to the creation of "Project Blind Awareness," which for many years was an innovative training program designed to enhance intuition in blind participants in order to help them become more mobile and independent. For years she also worked as a corporate educator and advisor to Fortune 500 businesses. Today Carol Ann remains just as convinced that people can be taught to work with and learn from their intuition in both their daily lives and their personal careers.

Carol Ann's book is both a valuable resource and guide to assist *any* individual interested in experiencing his or her personal psychic abilities. In addition to learning what ESP is and why you should develop it, Carol Ann takes you through easy-to-follow exercises that will enable you to relax, set aside the worries of your conscious mind, and simply become aware of the psychic impressions that have been around you all the time—you just may never have known how to look for them.

Whether it's seeing auras, learning how to scan energies, sensing the impressions that come from objects and pictures, working with healing, or "traveling" to any location with the imagination of your mind, Carol Ann Liaros' practical approaches to accessing personal intuition will be valuable to anyone (experienced or novice) interested in tapping into personal resources beyond the five senses.

In the end, what may make Carol Ann Liaros' work most notable of all is that in a very real sense it will provide personal experiences with the fact that there is much more to us than a physical body.

Kevin J. Todeschi
Executive Director and CEO
of Edgar Cayce's A.R.E. /Atlantic University
EdgarCayce.org

Introduction

The exercises in this book are designed to help you explore the development of your own intuition through personal experience and practice. Each of us has psychic abilities that can be developed and put into practical use in everyday life. If you're skeptical or think that psychic ability is something possessed by only a few, then you're at the exact same place where I once found myself. In fact, at one time I couldn't imagine having a psychic experience, let alone being a psychic!

Many years ago, in the midst of some personal challenges and questions about my life's direction, I went to see a psychic who had been recommended to me by a friend. Although I believed in the existence of intuition, I was certain that only a few individuals had access to psychic information. In spite of my friend's optimism about the insights I would receive from this particular psychic, I found after his reading that I felt convinced the information he had given me was not applicable to my life and was total nonsense.

During the course of the reading, he told me that I had psychic abilities and that I would be using these skills to teach others. In fact, he went on to say that I would be doing extensive traveling and working with "men in white coats, like doctors and scientists." He also stated that I would write a book about my experiences. I felt him inaccurate on every count. If this psychic had any legitimate abilities, I was certain that he had been having an "off" day.

After the reading, I left his office convinced that his words had no relevance for me. My skepticism was unshakable. However, my own cool reception about the psychic's reading was in stark contrast to the enthusiasm of some of my friends who had received readings from the very same individual. In fact, they were convinced that his information might be correct, and if I truly had a psychic talent, they wanted to see if they could get readings from me.

Although the thought seemed absolutely ridiculous, they were persistent and clearly excited about the idea of my being a psychic. Reluctantly, I agreed to attempt some readings about my friends, their lives, and some of the questions they had been dealing with. To my surprise, every time I did a reading, it turned out to be extremely accurate. However, I was able to rationally explain how my "readings" were no more than logical extensions of the things I already knew about their lives. None of these readings involved any real psychic ability on my part. I was still convinced that psychic ability was something only a few individuals possessed and that I wasn't one of them.

One day a friend showed up at my door with a shopping bag filled with items she had collected from a number of other people. She wanted me to touch each item and give a reading on its owner—which would prove once and for all whether I was psychic. The bag contained rings, watches, hairbrushes, photographs, and many other items. Obediently, I took each item, one by one. As I held it, I attempted to concentrate on the person who was connected with the object. In my mind, I "saw" fleeting images and pictures. Sometimes I "heard" words and phrases. And, on occasion, I simply "felt" subtle physical sensations. At times, these impressions were no more than gut feelings or hunches; somehow I would "know" something about the individual without knowing exactly how I knew. Throughout this experience, my friend wrote down each impression I gave her—though I was still convinced that the whole thing was just my imagination.

Finally, when the shopping bag was empty, we went back over each item to check it for accuracy. To my surprise, one by one, my impressions turned out to be true. No longer could I simply rationalize my experiences away. Later the thought struck me that *if, in fact, I really had psychic abilities, didn't everyone?*

Not too long after, I attended a lecture by the late Hugh Lynn Cayce, son of famed psychic Edgar Cayce, and then head of the Association for Research and Enlightenment, Inc. (A.R.E.) in Virginia Beach, Virginia. A series of meetings followed that would change my life's direction and put me on a totally new path. I spoke with Hugh Lynn about my experiences, and after the lecture, he introduced me to members of the Board of Directors of Rosary Hill College and to Dr. Justa Smith, a scientist, educator, and nun who was beginning to do research with healers.

During my work at the Institute I began showing friends and associate how to develop their own ESP, based upon my firsthand experiences. In time, I became more and more involved with psychic research, workshops, and readings that were being conducted with some of the most well-known healers and psychics in the world. The intervening years have proven quite interesting.

For decades I have given lectures and taught classes. I have worked with doctors and scientists, consulting and teaching courses that bridge parapsychology, medicine, and science. I have worked extensively with businesses and executives, helping individuals to understand the practical side of intuition, compassion, and community. I have traveled around the US and Canada, logging over 1,000,000 air miles! As I look back on that first reading when the psychic discussed my involvement with intuition and ESP, time has proven him accurate on every count.

When I first began my intuitive work, I must admit that some of my family and friends were not very pleased with the new direction my life had taken. They were afraid that because of my involvement with psychic phenomena, I might somehow lose touch with reality. Although I knew this wasn't true, I had difficulty convincing them. Over the years, I have discovered that this fear of losing touch with reality is common not only for those who are skeptical of ESP, but also for some individuals who are curious but hesitant about developing their own abilities.

In truth it would be more accurate to state that those individuals who develop their intuitive faculties are much more in touch with reality than those who do not. Modern physicists tell us that solid-appearing objects are not really solid at all; in a sense, the material world and our human bodies are illusory and transitory—something mystics have claimed all along. Individuals who develop psychic abilities learn to see the world as moving molecules or as vibrational fields of energy. Those who insist that the physical world is all that there is to see cannot perceive beyond the limits of their own illusion. Who, then, is really more in touch with reality? *Unlocking Your Intuition* will show you that there is much more to the real world than you ever knew existed.

"Psychic is of the Soul" 261-15
Edgar Cayce

Views of Intuitive or Psychic Experiences:

OLD PARADIGM	NEW PARADIGM
Woman "thing"	Everyone's "thing"
Without purpose	Purposeful
Little value	Valuable asset
Linear functioning	Quantum-leap experiencing
Unpredictable	Reliable
Inaccurate	Accurate
Capricious	On demand
Illogical	Translogical
Weird	Exciting possibilities
Find the "right" technique	Discover various avenues
Is not reliable	Can be reliable
Too "right brained"	Used in tandem with left brain
A "gift" for a select few	All have the "gift"
Either /or	Invokes parallel processing

1

Why Should I Develop My ESP?
And Just What Is It?

There is nothing difficult about developing ESP. In fact, it is such an easy and natural process that most of us simply overlook it. The most difficult task I have consistently faced in my workshops is convincing students how easy it is to use. Once that hurdle is passed, individuals are able to see some clear evidence of their own intuitive abilities.

The real question may be "Why develop your intuition at all?" Some individuals have cited very practical reasons, such as wanting to use it to help solve problems or for obtaining insights in order to make better decisions. Others hope to gain objectivity for setting realistic goals or perhaps in order to increase their own creativity. Many are interested in using ESP in their daily lives, in their personal situations, and at the workplace. Some people clearly want to help in understanding personal psychic experiences which may have started at a very early age. Regardless of the reasons, everyone can benefit from getting in touch with the intuitive capabilities which we all possess.

After forty-five years of experience, there is no question in my mind that developing ESP broadens self-understanding and brings people closer to one another. Many individuals see positive results in every area of their lives: physically, mentally, emotionally, and spiritually as soon as they begin working with the additional insights that intuition has to offer. In fact, psychic development offers a larger perspective on life and a new sense of connectedness with family, friends, and all of humanity.

Unfortunately, there is still a common misconception that intuitive experiences happen infrequently and only to a handful of "special" individuals. However, the truth is that most people have experienced extrasensory perception numerous times in their lives, and for many it is actually a very common experience. Regardless of how common it is, many people remain skeptical of psychic phenomena and most never seriously considered the thought that they may be psychic themselves.

I would describe people who are psychically aware in this way: they are warm, sociable, and easy going; they are quick, alert, and show their emotions easily; they are adventuresome and show enthusiasm for life; and they are practical and realistic. *In short, these are the very characteristics one would expect to find in any healthy, well-balanced individual.* All healthy, grounded individuals have the ability to utilize psychic information in their everyday lives. Those who are out of touch with this fact are ignoring one of life's adventures as well as an incredibly useful asset.

Most of us haven't begun to imagine the capacity of the human mind. Experts agree that we're using only a small fraction of our brain capacity, perhaps as little as five to twenty percent. Regardless of the percentage, it's an established fact that we are not using our full potential. Part of this untapped potential relates a heightened sensory system that each individual can become aware of through experience and training. It is something that everyone can develop because psychic awareness is not so much a *thing* as it is a *process*. Intuition makes use of the intellect and the imagination—both attributes of the brain. To understand how it works, it is helpful to understand how the brain functions.

Some of the earliest brain research was done with individuals who had suffered brain damage through accidents or illness. Researchers discovered that the two hemispheres of the brain controlled not only different sides of the body but also different brain functions. The left hemisphere controls the right side of the body and is involved with rational, analytical thought processes, for example language and mathematics. The right hemisphere controls the left side of the body and specializes in spatial and holistic functions, integrating many operations at once. Imagination, visualization, and psychic processes are all examples of right-brain functioning.

Neither hemisphere of the brain is smarter nor more advanced than the other. But in most individuals it is common to see one hemisphere more developed than the other. Ways in which connections between the left and right hemispheres can be accomplished include relaxation and meditation, creative imagery, intuition and laughter. The exercises in *Unlocking Your Intuition* can assist individuals in integrating the left and right hemispheres of their brain as they learn to balance the functions of the intellect, the imagination, and the intuitive processes. The result can be a more fully integrated, balanced personality and a balanced-brain individual, who can be more successful both personally and professionally. And, as an individual works at such integration, psychic or extrasensory information can be made extremely practical as well as much more readily accessible.

In my experience I have found that working in groups of two or more is one of the most productive environments for beginning students of ESP. A shared experience seems to enhance the process, for students learn as much from each other as they do from the material. Also, another person or a group provides immediate, direct feedback and support, which makes the whole experience more enjoyable. However, *Unlocking Your Intuition* does provide exercises for practicing on your own, and many of the group exercises can easily be adapted to try alone as well.

Psychic processes know no boundaries of space and time. Therefore, the impressions you receive may concern events from the past, the present, or the future. Precognition involves knowledge of future events obtained through psychic means. Retrocognition, on the other hand, involves having or perceiving knowledge of the past through the intuitive processes.

Although the advantages of obtaining psychic insights into the future are innumerable and obvious, the ability to obtain knowledge about the past is also quite useful. Archeologists have used it to help locate buried sites and gain information about artifacts and ancient civilizations. The police have used it to help solve criminal cases and find missing persons. Mental health professionals often use retrocognition in therapy with clients who may need to remember past events and experiences that have been repressed or forgotten. Retrocognition also allows for the ability to see into past lives.

You should be aware that retrocognition and precognition impressions may be experienced through clairvoyance, clairaudience, or clairsentience. For information about future events, try concentrating on moving ahead in time. For information from the past, concentrate on moving back.

As you can see, there is more than one way to receive information psychically. A common misperception is that all psychics are clairvoyant, receiving most of their impressions visually. This isn't always the case. In a typical reading, various impressions of all kinds may be perceived.

For example, I once gave a reading for a Chicago man who had come to me for a consultation. As I concentrated on him, I saw three arrows connecting him to three foreign countries. I wasn't sure what countries were represented, but I told him my impression and he offered to get me an atlas from the next room to help identify the locales. As he got up, I heard these words spoken silently:

"India, France, and England." As I concentrated on his next question concerning his connections with those countries, I had strong feeling responses that provided the additional information he requested. I felt that his lifelong dream was to go India, that his ring was from France, and that he would be making a business trip to England. The man confirmed each of my feelings and in fact, stated that he would probably have to go to England within six months since he was collaborating on a book with an individual from that country.

This is a typical example of the kinds of psychic impressions you may receive in a reading, all in a very short span of time. In this case, the first impression was clairvoyant (symbols representing arrows and foreign countries). The next impression was clairaudient (the words "India, France, and England" spoken in a thought). The final impressions were clairsentient (an inner knowledge about his connections with each country).

The intuitive process utilizes unconscious material and brings it to conscious levels of awareness. However, when a barrier exists between these levels of awareness, it can be more difficult to obtain the information. Fear, tension, and interference by the intellect are all barriers to the unconscious mind; these are also the most common problems experienced by individuals beginning to work with their ESP.

Some people are afraid to contact the unconscious mind. They may have had negative or frightening psychic experiences as children, or they have learned to be frightened of them from parents or religious authorities who believed that it was "the work of the devil." At the root of this fear is the belief that psychic processes are uncontrollable and therefore dangerous; the fear in losing control is a problem only if an individual is unbalanced emotionally or if he chooses for it to be a problem. The exercises in this book are all safe and manageable; at no time will you be out of control of your experience. Throughout all of these exercises you will be in complete control and have the choice to turn on and turn off the psychic process at will. Many priests, nuns, ministers, doctors, health care professionals, business people, parents, students, and children have been able to make personal intuition extremely practical, benefitting greatly from their own psychic abilities in the process.

There are many ways to develop intuitive abilities. The exercises here offer an approach I've been using for over forty-five years in workshops and training programs. These techniques have proven themselves again and again. They offer a wide range of learning experiences. Some of them will appeal to you more than others. I encourage you *to find and use the techniques that work best for you.* Although you may find that you are more naturally adept at one more than another, it is to your benefit to develop all of your psychic senses.

And one more thing: it's important to have fun while you're exploring your intuition. It is a process of self-discovery, personal unfoldment, and nearly limitless insight.

No matter how you accomplish it, practice is the most important technique for developing your intuitive skills. There are always a few students who attempt one or two psychic exercises and then give up, claiming they knew they were not really psychic to begin with. Yet, many more individuals have gone on to master the very techniques with which they had little or no success on their first attempts. Practice is what makes the difference. Learning to relax and tune into the psychic processes can take some time, but the rewards will be well worth the effort.

> "You are an individualized, segmented part of Universal Mind,
> And as such are connected on subconscious levels with all minds."
> Harold Sherman

Vocabulary

In order to gain an understanding of the psychic process itself, it will be helpful to explore some of the words associated with intuitive experiences. These words will provide valuable background for some of the experiential exercises you will be attempting later.

Aura relates to the subtle energy field that appears to emanate from both animate and inanimate objects and can provide intuitive information about the subject itself. The vibrational patterns within the aura are multicolored and multilayered. It is visible through intuitive means as well as through Kirlian photography.

Clairaudience means "clear hearing." It can be as if someone were talking into your ear or can also be experienced as a thought. Words, numbers, or whole sentences may be perceived in this way. Practice will help you to distinguish between thoughts that are the product of your intellect and imagination or actual clairaudient impressions.

Clairsentience means "clear sensing." Gut feelings and hunches are examples of clairsentience. Another example would be a physical sensation experienced during a reading that relates to the individual's state of health or emotional condition. If the feeling or hunch concerns a future event, it is called *precognition*.

Clairvoyance means "clear seeing." It is the faculty of psychic sight. As you practice ESP, you may perceive visual impressions that are similar to seeing images or pictures in your imagination. Clairvoyant impressions can appear as moving images like an imaginary movie, or they may be still pictures like a photograph. The images often appear in symbolic form, and learning to interpret these symbols correctly is perhaps the greatest challenge of clairvoyance.

ESP or Extrasensory Perception means having access to information which is not perceptible by the five ordinary senses of sight, sound, taste, touch, and smell.

HSP or Higher Sense Perception is another term for ESP. The terms have the same meaning, but higher sense perception suggests the existence of a finer, more subtle sense perception that more accurately describes the psychic process.

Intuition Intuitives just "know" the information. They do not see, hear, feel, smell, or taste the information; they just "know" it. When asked how they got an impression, quite often they will shrug and say "I just knew it." These people are quite often accused early in life as being "know–it–alls."

Kirlian photography is a method of photographing the aura.

Mediumship or Channeling is the phenomenon of a spirit (a dis-incarnate—a deceased individual) communicating through a living person. Mediums contact the disincarnate or a "guide" takes over the mediums and speaks through them. There can be dangers associated with mediumship, such as possession.

Parapsychology is the field of study dealing with psychic phenomena. Researchers and scientists have conducted parapsychological research in biology, psychology, medicine, engineering, and other fields.

Precognition involves knowledge of future events through psychic processes or intuition.

PSI is a term that scientists use instead of "psychic" or "psychic phe-nomena."

Psychic Phenomena is the general phrase for paranormal events and abilities that cannot be explained in terms of established scientific principles. It includes ESP, psychokinesis (PK), mediumship, and other phenomena.

Psychic is someone who receives information from beyond the five physical senses of seeing, hearing, feeling, smelling, or tasting.

Psychokinesis (PK) also referred to as telekinesis. It is the influence of mind over matter—the ability to move or influence objects by thought. Spoon bending and table tipping are examples of this phenomenon.

Remote Viewing is the term used to gather information from a distance without the use of the five senses.

Retrocognition involves having or perceiving knowledge of the past through psychic or intuitive means.

Telepathy is mind–to–mind communication, more commonly known as "mind reading." Telepathy, which is not to be confused with clairaudience, involves direct contact with another person's thoughts. Telepathic communication may be perceived word for word or as a general impression. Some individuals are better at sending telepathic thoughts, while others at receiving them.

Suggestions When Visiting a Psychic

- Every person has his or her own area of expertise. If possible, find out if it is relationships, precognition, retrocognition, locating lost objects, etc. What are your needs?

- Make a list of questions to cover everything you want to know. Some people are nervous or intrigued with information the psychic gives them and may leave with questions unanswered.

- Be prepared: If the psychic does psychometry, have all of your objects ready. Follow the instructions of the psychic. Allow the reader to proceed in his or her own manner. Record the reading. Sometimes we hear what we want to hear, not what was said. Also, you can check the accuracy of the psychic to discover what areas he or she has been most accurate for *you*. (Be concerned if the person will not allow taping.)

- Do not send telepathic messages. You will not want your fears/ guesses/wishes fed back to you.

- Be courteous, even if you are a skeptic. The individual deserves to be treated with consideration. As the psychic is concentrating, do not rattle papers, smoke, squirm in your seat, interrupt, or display other distracting behaviors.

- Do not press for information. The psychic will give you everything he or she receives. A good reading is designed to help you cope with your life.

- Be discerning. Not critical.

- Keep an open mind—but not a sieve!

- Remember the percentage of accuracy varies with each psychic. Get the perspective of friends whose judgment you trust to review the reading with you. Sometimes our blind spots interfere with our evaluation!

- Inaccuracies can occur in readings if the psychic is reading your mind (telepathy) or misinterpreting information he or she receives. It can be a good idea to ask *how the person* receives the information. You may recognize the information while he or she may be inter- preting from his or her own experiences. Be willing to verify.

- After the reading is completed, share the information that you can verify. Psychics are human and feedback can be very helpful for them. If the psychic makes predictions, it would be very thoughtful to write and let the person know the outcome.

- Do not try to prolong the reading beyond the agreed-upon time limit.

- Do not expect the psychic to remember your reading—and maybe even you!

2

Relaxation and Concentration:
The First Lesson

Since tension and interference by the intellect are the most common barriers to the psychic processes, relaxation and concentration are the most important keys to using your ESP. Intuitive impressions are subtle and sometimes elusive. Too much tension acts as a kind of anesthetic that numbs your sensitivity to higher levels of awareness. This static blocks your sensitive feelings. Relaxation, on the other hand, increases your sensitivity to physical and mental perception of all kinds. In fact, each of your intuition exercises should begin with some type of a relaxation technique, such as the one offered in this chapter.

As you explore your own intuition, it will become clear why relaxing the body and concentrating the mind are so important. But in addition to developing ESP, there are many more good reasons for relaxation and concentration. One is stress reduction. Stress is one of the major causes of physical, mental, and emotional disease. Excessive stress on the body and the nervous system can result in imbalance, often leading to illness, bodily disorders, and even premature death. In the last few decades, society has recognized this problem and has responded with increased emphasis on "wellness" programs, physical exercise, yoga, and meditation.

In addition to quieting the mind and relaxing the body, relaxation techniques have positive effects upon an individual's physical health and mental/emotional well-being. In many ways, relaxation is similar to the practice of meditation, which has been scientifically proven to be beneficial. Individuals who practice meditation regularly experience a calm and relaxed state of body and mind, renewed vitality, mental alertness, and increased concentration. They feel less stress in their lives and seem to cope better when stressful situations arise. Meditators also report having more restful sleep patterns or require less sleep to begin with.

Psychologists who have studied meditation have found regular meditators to be happier, more relaxed, and often able to demonstrate more openness and empathy in their relationships than individuals who don't meditate. Meditation has also proven to be effective in curing or improving physical and mental disorders such as ulcers, allergies, asthma, depression, anxiety, arthritis, and even epileptic seizures.

Developing ESP, like practicing meditation, requires more than relaxation. It requires concentration. I define concentration as *keen, one-pointed attention*. It is the process of focusing the content of your awareness to such a fine point that it is able to break through to an even higher finer level of sensitivity. Like relaxation, concentration involves letting go. It involves releasing all of the thoughts and the worries that preoccupy your mind and instead focusing your attention upon a single object of concentration. As you learn to let go of the tension in your body and mind while focusing your attention on the matter at hand, you will find that intuitive exercises are easier and much more fun than you imagined.

Although this may sound labor-intensive, working with your intuition is actually a lot simpler than the ways in which we normally attempt to accomplish something. In fact, I find it much easier to simply relax and concentrate on what I need to know or gently focusing upon what problem I need to solve (allowing the process of ESP to do the work for me) rather than feeling as though I must "DO" something. I sometimes say, "ESP is for lazy people." And by lazy, I don't mean being irresponsible or doing nothing; I mean *doing things in an easy, relaxed man-*

ner. Many of us have a difficult time with relaxing because we are taught that to be productive, worthwhile individuals we have to struggle and work very hard. I enjoy working, but because I often do things in an easier fashion, I have the time and energy to enjoy myself, no matter what activity I'm involved in.

It is helpful for the intuitive process to include a relaxation and concentration exercise before every ESP exercise. Two exercises, one long and one shorter version, are included here for you to try. The longer exercise can be used at the beginning of any intuitive session and the shorter version can be used before beginning any other techniques you might choose to explore during the session. It is not so important what techniques you use, but it is important that you take time out for some kind of relaxation before attempting any exercise.

The technique I use the most often involves tensing and relaxing the body's major muscle groups. Tensing and relaxing your muscles helps you to relax and let go while facilitating your concentration by focusing your attention on specific areas of your body. As you relax, you will become much more aware of your body and your physical environment, and you may even begin to notice small physical discomforts that you were not aware of before. For example, you may find that you are sitting in an uncomfortable position or that your nose has started to itch. Your clothing may feel tight or restricting, or you may become aware of the pressure of your watch, ring, or earrings. Perhaps your shoes will feel like they are pinching your feet. The first thing to do is to attend to all of your distractions so that they are no longer there. Change positions or find a more comfortable chair. Remove your jewelry. Slip out of your shoes. Loosen your collar or belt. Take the time you need in order to make yourself feel as comfortable as possible.

As you begin, you may also become aware of all of the little distractions in your environment. Little sounds that you were not really aware of in your normal conscious state may become amplified to the point where they are annoying. When I find this happening to me, I mentally travel around to all the sounds and put them into an imaginary box with a volume control knob on it. When I have collected all of the sounds in the box, I mentally turn down the volume control knob until the sounds no longer bother me. In time, you may discover your own methods of tuning out environmental distractions; whatever works for you is fine. The important thing is to remember not to ignore the distractions but instead to attend to them in some way so that you can go beyond them. If you find your attention wandering during the exercise, simply bring it back very gently to your own breathing or to a single point of focus within yourself.

It doesn't matter if you sit in a chair, on a pillow, or lie down on the floor to relax, but it may be best to sit in a straight back chair so that you do not fall asleep during the relaxation experience.

There are several ways to conduct this exercise. If you are practicing with a group, have someone read the exercise aloud or pretape the exercise on a recording device. If you are not in a position to record your own CD, you may wish for someone else to read through the exercise for you slowly, or you could read it through yourself beforehand and then do the exercise mentally, one muscle group at a time.

If someone is leading the relaxation exercise, here are a few tips. First, be sure that the person is relaxed. Tension and nervousness can be communicated through one's voice and behavior. On the other hand, a calm and relaxed manner will be expressed quite naturally to others. Secondly, be sure to present the exercise in a slow, steady, gentle manner, pausing as indicated. Finally, allow plenty of time for the exercise. Those who are new to this may need more time than others. In the beginning, fifteen to twenty minutes may be appropriate in order to become truly relaxed. Later, with experience, you may find that five to seven minutes is quite long enough.

At the close of the exercise, see how long you can recall or maintain this relaxed state of body and mind—an hour, a day, a week, or even longer. Whenever you feel yourself becoming tense or anxious, practice the relaxation experience again and feel its calming positive effects. When you've accomplished the relaxation technique, feel free to move onto the first intuitive experience, which is *Energy Sensing*.

> **"Inner conflict between left and right**
> **Brain processes may reflect out into**
> **The world as prejudice."**
> **Carol Ann Liaros**

Relaxation and Concentration

(Long version)

This exercise is important because it will encourage you to set aside a total reliance upon the left-brain logical thought processes and through the process of relaxation, facilitate the activities of your own imagination, creativity, and receptivity. In addition, relaxation helps to connect the left and right brains for more balanced functioning.

This is an exercise to help you relax and concentrate. Sit comfortably, with your feet flat on the floor and your hands upon your lap; then close your eyes.

Take a slow, deep, even breath, filling your abdomen to capacity, and hold it to a count of three. One . . . Two . . . Three . . .

Breathe out very slowly through your mouth . . . and tell yourself to relax . . .

Take another slow, deep, even breath, filling the abdomen to capacity, and hold it to a count of three. One . . . Two . . . Three . . .

Very slowly, breathe out through your mouth. Gently telling yourself to relax, knowing that your body follows the commands of your mind . . .

Take another slow, deep, even breath and hold it to a count of three . . . One . . . Two . . . Three . . .

Breathe out through the mouth . . . very gently telling yourself to relax . . .

Now tense up the muscles in your feet by curling your toes and making them as tight and taut as you can. For a moment, hold this tension . . .

Now relax those muscles . . .

And relax them even more . . .

Tense up the muscles in your lower legs, making those muscles as tense and taut as you can . . .

Tense them even more . . . and feel that tension with your body and mind . . .

Now relax . . . and tell those muscles to relax even more . . . .

Tense the muscles in your abdomen and lower back . . . tense them even more . . . and relax . . .

Now tell yourself to relax those muscles even more . . . and feel the relaxation with your body and mind.

Now, tense up the muscles in the upper part of your torso by hunching up both shoulders.

Tense the muscles in the back and chest . . . and feel this tension with your body and your mind.

Now relax those muscles . . . and relax them even more . . .

Tense up the muscles in both arms by clenching your fists. Make hard, tight fists and feel all the muscles in your arms become very tense and taut . . .

And slowly relax . . . relax them just a bit more . . .

Now tense up every muscle in your face that you can, particularly around your eyes . . . Press your tongue against the roof of your mouth and crease your brow . . . make all the muscles in your face and head feel very tense and taut.

Now relax . . . relax the eyes, the tongue, the jaw, the forehead, and relax those muscles even more . . . feel this relaxation with your body and your mind.

Now tense every muscle in your body, beginning with the toes and going up through the legs . . . the abdomen and lower back . . . the chest and shoulders . . . the arms and hands . . . and the face . . .

Now tense up all the muscles in your body even more, and feel this tension in every muscle . . .

Now, very slowly, as though you were moving in slow motion, relax every muscle in your body . . . slowly and gently . . . relax every muscle . . .

Now slowly, let your head fall forward and gently rotate your head and neck in one direction and then the other. Tell yourself to relax . . .

Tell the muscles to let go . . . communicate to every cell in your body to relax even more. Feel the relaxation with your body and your mind. Be aware of the feeling of relaxation throughout your body . . .

Now take your mind, or your imagination, to the top of your head and take your mind on a trip down through your physical body. When you come to a muscle that is not relaxed, tense up that muscle, hold it, making it as tight and tense as you can, and then finally relax that muscle. Do as many muscles as is necessary to release the stress from your body.

Let your mind seek out those tense muscles . . . and relax them . . .

Communicate to every cell, in every muscle of your entire body to relax even more . . .

(Longer pause)

Now, in your imagination, visualize a funnel coming out of the top of your head and reaching into infinity. If you cannot visualize it, feel it. Know it is there. Visualize or feel a cleansing, purifying, healing white light pouring down through the funnel and flowing into the top of your head . . .

In your imagination, visualize this cleansing, purifying healing energy filling your head and flowing down into your neck . . . into your upper body . . . down your arms and into your hands and fingers . . . feel this energy flowing into your abdomen . . . into your legs and down into your feet and toes . . .

In your imagination, visualize or feel this energy cleansing, purifying, and healing your entire body . . . experience yourself so filled with this energy that it is radiating out of every pore in your body . . . the energy is cleansing, purifying, and healing the outside of your body, and your energy field, and aura as well . . .

In your imagination, visualize your aura. Feel the energy of your aura. Know that it is there . . .

Now, in your mind or imagination, expand your aura so that it radiates three feet from your body. You might experience this as you would blow up a balloon. With each breath, the aura gets larger and larger. Experience your energy field expanding.

Expand your aura even more so that it radiates eight feet from your body . . . visualize it, feel it, or simply know that it is there . . .

And with your mind, expand your aura so that it fills the entire room. Experience your aura as completely as you can . . . feel it, visualize it, and know that it is there . . . .

Now, let yourself relax, allowing the aura to return to its normal size . . .

Take a slow, deep, even breath, filling your abdomen to capacity, and breathing out through your mouth . . . tell yourself that when you open your eyes, you will maintain a completely relaxed state of body and mind.

Take another deep breath and open your eyes.

Relaxation and Concentration
(Short version)

Tense up every muscle in your body, beginning with the toes and going up through the legs . . . the abdomen and lower back . . . the chest and shoulders . . . and the face . . .

Now, very slowly, as though you were moving in slow motion, relax every muscle in your body . . . slowly and gently . . . relax every muscle . . .

Now slowly, let your head fall forward and gently rotate your head and neck in one direction and then the other. Tell yourself to relax . . .
Tell the muscles to let go . . . communicate to every cell in your body to relax even more. Experience the relaxation with your body and your mind.

Take a deep breath . . . open your eyes . . . maintaining that very relaxed state of mind and body.

PROCESSING
Relaxation and Concentration

Process what happened with this technique. What did you experience? What caught your attention?	What worked? What energized you? What were the low points? What frustrated you?	What has been your most significant learning? What are the implications of this learning?	What are some of the ways you could use this technique in your life?

3

Seven Keys to Unlocking Your Intuition

Having given readings for forty-five years, I have discovered there are certain formulas that work. I am sharing these formulas in the Seven Keys; these keys will be helpful as you learn to use your intuitive skills.

Key Number One-Relaxation

Research has shown that the more relaxed one is the keener the sight, meaning one observes and notices more—the peripheral vision is extended, the sense of hearing is more acute as is the sense of smell, taste, and touch. ESP, or intuition, is an extension of the senses, so the results of relaxation also hold true when you want to become aware of another level of reality. We are swimming in a sea of higher, finer energy anywhere we go. We are constantly bombarded by all kinds of waves: radio waves, TV waves, microwaves, as well as the energy field of each person we encounter.

In order to become aware of this level of reality, the more relaxed one is the more sensitive a person is to these vibrations. When I first started in this field in 1996, scientists would say to me, "Carol Ann, don't use words like vibrations; they sound very esoteric." But, of course, what science has discovered is that everything is vibration. Consequently, when one wants or needs to become aware of this other reality, a shift in focus to this higher, finer level of reality is possible by becoming relaxed. For a person who is usually relaxed, this isn't going to be a difficult step. Anyone who practices yoga, tai chi, or some kind of relaxation or hypnotherapy may be able to relax easily. For a tense person, one who has been under a lot of stress or one who is extremely analytical, the use of some type of relaxation technique is advised. The technique used with this course is a relaxation response brought about by tensing and relaxing your muscles. Research indicates you only have to do this technique approximately twenty–one times; and after that, when you say "relax," your body will relax. The body follows your command. In the beginning, you go through this process step by step; however, after a while, the step–by–step process is not necessary. Learning to ride a two–wheel bicycle is a similar process. At first, you used training wheels, your parents stood beside you, and you rode on a smooth surface; but you didn't spend the rest of your life riding a two wheeler that way. After you learned to balance, all of these conditions were not required. As with repeating "relaxation" to yourself several times, awareness of this higher, finer level of energy and interpretation of these vibrations become possible. It is one thing to feel them, experience, and/or see them; but if the vibrations cannot be interpreted, they are not very useful. Part of the training in this course is to interpret energies.

In times of stress, extreme stress, some people have become very psychic. This is the other end of the spectrum from relaxation. At one end of this spectrum is relaxation, and at the other end is stress which can also produce altered states of consciousness. However, stress is not the healthy way to achieve an altered state. Putting yourself under stress to become intuitive or psychic is not advisable! This course will teach relaxation, a healthy method to use to tap into your psychic abilities.

Key Number Two—Concentration

Another word for concentration could be "focused." Concentration is important as you are tuning into a situation or a person because only specific information is needed. For example, there is not a need to know that five months ago this person started a new cycle in life, is going to sell the house, and move. If you own your own business, want to hire someone, and have three résumés in front of you, how do you know which person is best suited for the position. Most people know how to write résumés; consequently, the three applicants may look equally qualified. Then comes the interview, and each applicant puts on his or her best face. How do you get the information you really need to know about these people that, more than likely, you can't ask them? Of course, none of them will put on résumé this fact: "Well, I'm really looking for a temporary stopgap before I go on to the company I'm waiting to hear from, but I really want the experience with your company for six months." Because that information is available at some level to everyone, you can use your intuition to access this fact and discover that this person is qualified but does not plan to stay. Without this information, you may have invested a great deal of money in the person's development. A question that the applicants wouldn't know the answer to might be: "Will this person get along with the other people in the office?" Questions such as this are important and need to be answered. The applicants won't know the answer, but you can. In concentration, you can be like a laser beam with the intent: *"This is the information I want."* If you're a doctor, you want medical information; if you're a lawyer, you want legal information; if you're a personnel manager, you want personnel information; if you're a parent, the information you need will be different.

Concentration has very practical applications for the selection of information needed. It can be compared to a radio. You want a particular station; you turn the dial to get that station. When you learn to concentrate—like a laser beam—you focus and get the information you want or need. When I want information on the stock market, I believe that I'm tuning into the collective minds and decisions of the people in the investing world. I sense the direction of their investments when I want to invest in the stock. You may not want to know the whole history of the stock; you do want to know how it will be doing at any given time: Is it going up? How high? Is it going down? How far down? You want specific information.

The way other people teach interests me, so I participate in other people's intuitive workshops. It is very interesting to hear about the same subject from many different perspectives. In some of the work-shops, the presenters would say "Open yourself up and let anything come in." There was no focusing on "This is the information I want." For most of us, the "honing in" on needed information is the most practical approach.

Learning a few simple concentration techniques will be valuable to you as you seek pertinent information and will also make it easier to get the information. One technique is to turn your attention to the middle of your forehead, keep it there; when you feel your attention wandering, very gently bring it back again and again no matter how many times your attention wanders. Continue this for two or three minutes. This technique is said to stimulate the third eye or our ability to see psychically. Another method is to concentrate on your breathing. By working with these two simple techniques, you are learning focused concentration in a relaxed state.

Key Number Three—Meditation

I consider meditation to be very important in psychic development. Although you do not have to meditate to be extremely intuitive, medi-tation keeps the spiritual components in the attunement and keeps one attuned to whatever higher power that person acknowledges. Medita-tion is important for spiritual growth and for keeping balanced. Some people come to a workshop and suddenly feel their intuition is their primary focus; one result can be that some of them may neglect their spouse and children, leave their job, and may engage in other types of destructive behavior. Meditation would help them stay balanced and keep their perspective so that the lenses in their glasses remain clear. In this way their intuition will fit, but won't overtake, their lives.

A person can be highly intuitive, give very accurate readings, and yet show little spirituality in his or her life. I have seen some psychics give readings and through their readings manipulate people. Linking with the Divine through meditation will assist you in keeping your behavior and actions geared toward the best outcome for yourself and for others.

Key Number Four—Keep a Journal

Now why would I tell you to keep a journal? Let me share with you what I did for many years. I had a notebook that I carried with me practically everywhere I went to record spontaneous impressions. I'd be driving and something would flash in; as soon as I could, I'd write in my notebook, recording the date, the time, and my impressions, *not my interpretations* of my impressions. Did I see a flash of a white uniform and smell a smell like antiseptic, and then feel this bustling activity? My *interpretation* might be that I am seeing a hospital and a nurse. However, the first thing I do is write down the *impressions* as I perceived them.

Before I went to bed, I would meditate for a short while and ask myself questions such as: "What will be happening of significance in the city of Buffalo, NY in the next thirty days?" I would wait for the impressions to come and write them down. Then I would continue with questions such as: "What is going to happen of significance in New York state in the next thirty days?" and record my impressions. I would continue by posing questions about the country and the globe and record my impressions. Also, I would ask about a friend, having received in advance "carte blanche" to tune into him or her at any time.

The next day when the volunteers came into the office, I would tell them what was written in my journal. Because I didn't watch television, didn't read the newspaper, didn't listen to the radio, many of the things recorded could happen, and I wouldn't be aware that they had happened. Since the volunteers knew this, they would monitor the news. I left space in my notebook for feedback. When I received the feedback, I would record it in that space. I would put in the article and underline the parts that were accurate comparing my impressions and my interpretation of my impressions.

This helps in many different ways. One, it will help you learn the difference between a wish, a fear, your imagination, a guess, or a psychic impression. You may find you have several impressions about a car accident, and you record them in your notebook. The car accident never happens! Other things do, but those don't. You begin to get a clear picture that this may be a fear, not an intuition. This process helps to distinguish between these experiences. Record the content of the intuition or the basic message; then write how it appeared. Was it vivid, clear, or somewhat clear? Was it far away or close? Was it well-defined or hazy? Some people experience a clear and defined image as an intuitive one; others, because they are visual and have such a good imagination, find when the image is fuzzy, they have an intuition. When they get a clear and defined impression, they are experiencing imagination. Again we all receive our intuitive impressions differently.

Keeping a journal helps you to learn how to judge your timing. When you get an impression and write it down, record the date, the time, the impressions, your interpretation, and wait to see what happens. When the event happens, look in your journal, and check the date you received the impression; for illustration purposes, let's say you recorded it on February 15. The event that you were writing about then happened thirty days later. It is important to watch that type of pattern. Some people get impressions shortly before an event; others far in advance. With the aid of your journal, you begin to know your timing. Paying attention to where you receive the information is also important. Was it right up in your face, in your head, outside your body? How far away or how close was it? When the event occurs (you may have seen it to the right), it happened in thirty days from the recorded intuition. This may lead you to wonder if you see the image to the right; does it mean it's going to happen in thirty days? A pattern of timing is evolving.

Time is one of the areas where mistakes frequently occur because there is no time. Often the event you learn about from a psychic is correct, but the timing is inaccurate. By journalizing, observing, and checking your impressions, you hone the skill of timing. By paying attention to where you get your impressions, where you see, or feel, or know, you can recognize how you receive future events. When I see or feel them slightly to the left that is the past; when they are to the right, they tend to be about the future, directly in front of me is the present. Some people discover the opposite is true for them.

Keeping a journal will help keep you balanced and humble. When doing readings, some people have a tendency to remember the correct answers and forget the misses; others are at the opposite end of the spectrum. They remember all the things that were wrong and don't remember what was right until their friends say, "Oh, don't you remember, you said . . . ." There it is in black and white in your journal and can be an accuracy barometer of your abilities. The psychic arena is one in which it is easy to get too egotistical or self-deluded; it is a field in which there can be a great deal of self-delusion. If you are doing really well and people are extremely complimentary, it is very easy to lose your perspective and become egotistical. However, if you have a record of your impressions, review your journal notes, and are aware of which impressions were correct and of which ones were not correct, you will discover the areas in which your accuracy seems to be higher. Just because someone is psychic doesn't mean he or she is accurate in all areas. Most people tend to be more accurate in the areas in which they are interested.

As I was keeping this notebook, one of my discoveries was that I seem to be skillful in precognition. In a scientific experiment that lasted for two years, I was tested and was found to be 93 to 97% accurate when predicting the future. However, I became interested in the 7% inaccuracy. Why aren't readings 100% accurate? I discovered there are many reasons for inaccuracy. Some of the reasons are the following: the future can be changed; the way you are feeling that day affects accuracy; negative ions in the air stimulate psychic ability. The scientists kept records of moon phases, and it became obvious that during a full moon my scores went up; my accuracy also increased when I had my period! All my friends wanted a reading when there was a full moon, and I had my period! There are many things that influence accuracy.

As you keep this notebook, you will learn your own symbols—some symbols are universal and some are personal. I also found my attitude about the readings was influential in the accuracy. When you have an aversion to a person and still make the heart connection, you get in touch with the soul; negativity disappears and probably won't interfere in the reading at all.

Key Number Five—Be a People Watcher

Being a people watcher is a characteristic many psychics seem to share, and an erroneous assumption held by most was that everyone was a people watcher! I became aware that wasn't necessarily true when I was sent to Jean Houston's institute in Pomona, NY, where she was going to train two of us for three days. A woman, an architect, who also worked at The Human Dimensions Institute and I were chosen to go. After participating in some exercises, Jean gave each of us the thesis for her next PhD. She explained that we were to symbolically change places by doing everything the way the other person did them. We went to dinner where I proceeded to sit in the corner so I could see the door. The conversation went something like this with my friend asking "Why are you sitting there?" and my reply "I like to see the door." "Why do you like to see the door?" "I like to see the people come in." "Why do you like to see the people come in?" Now I'm getting exasperated! "Well, don't you?" I asked. "I like to look at them. You know you can tell by the look on their face and the way they hold themselves, if they are happy, or sad, or angry." She wanted to know why I cared. I explained that I like to make up a story about the people I see. For example, this person looks angry, and I make up a story about her. She had a fight with her sister, and because they are in business together, it's affecting the business and the family. She replied "I never heard of that!" At that point, I wanted to know what she did. She explained she sits with her back to the door so she will not be distracted from the person with whom she is talking. I couldn't believe it! In order to follow Jean's instructions, she had me sit with my back to the door while she sat facing the door. She watched the people come in and made up stories about them. We both had difficulty in our changed positions.

As we walked from the restaurant to the motel, she asked me: "How do you walk back to the hotel?" A little apprehensive now, I said "What do you mean how do I walk back to the hotel? Well, it is a beautiful night so I feel the air, and I smell the trees, and I sort of 'float' back." Tonight I wasn't going to do that! I had to be her and get into my body, smell the air, fill my lungs, and feel my muscles moving. I thought: *Oh, this is going to be a very bad night.* I had to stride back while she had to "float"; it was equally difficult for her. Upon arriving at the hotel, she inquired how I would read Jean's manuscript. Now I'm afraid to tell her! Finally I replied "I would take a nice hot bubble bath, get in my night gown, climb into my bed, and read it." She replied that she would sit up in a chair, fully clothed, so she wouldn't fall asleep. She would be alert. Needless to say, she had to take the bubble bath, and I sat up to stay alert!

In order to practice, since we all find ourselves in lines sometime at the bank, at the grocery store, in the airport, as well as other places, the question arises "What do you do?" Try looking at people and make up stories. Much of the process is visual observation and intellectual deduction. The way a person looks, stands, holds her mouth, the look in her eye, how tight her muscles are will tell you a lot about the person. There's nothing psychic about that at all. However, go on with the story in your imagination. She may look very relaxed or she may look happy. The story might be she is getting money out of the bank to go on vacation. It doesn't matter if it's true or not! At this point you are activating and stimulating your imagination, and the imagination flows into intuitive or psychic impressions. You don't "look at" people, but you "see" them. It's a very different thing. "Looking at" someone is an outer observation; "seeing" someone is an inner process that apparently leads to accurate intuitive impressions.

Key Number Six—Join a Group

Join a group of like-minded people whatever that might be—a *Search for God* group, a meditation group, or a psychic development group. One of the things I feel uncomfortable about is when I hear someone declare "This is the way and the only way." "This is the book, the only book. Don't read anything other than Edgar Cayce and don't believe anything other than Lazarus, or others." I encourage people to read books on the subject in which they are interested and know there are going to be diametrically opposite ideas to what they believe at this time. This makes them think!

Over the years I have observed people from a dogmatic religious background come in the intuitive arena and become as dogmatic about intuitive/psychic/spiritual issues as they had been in their religious beliefs. A smorgasbord is out there; taste it all, and then you can sift the wheat from the shaft for yourself. For your development in this incarnation, this is what works; this is what makes sense; this is what's comfortable. When you read something that is exactly the opposite of what you believe, new light is shed on that subject, and you might become stronger and add a new dimension to your beliefs. Reading material that opposes what you believe supports your spiritual growth and assists in keeping beliefs in perspective. Even if you are in a *Search for God* group and everyone is following the same book, there may be twelve people who have probably twelve different perspectives on the same chapter. One isn't right and one wrong—just different. It is healthy psychologically, mentally, and spiritually to hear or read other perspectives. It doesn't mean you have to agree with them. Another benefit is this type of activity helps you to be less autocratic.

Some people do really well at workshops. They are accurate in what they do and become recognized for that accuracy. The temptation to become egotistical is a possibility. One reason may be that they don't have people around them who kid and joke with them. If they did, it would help keep their feet on the ground. It's advisable to belong to a group which experiments with intuition because as everyone practices a technique, you discover you might get 98% right, someone else gets 60% while another person gets 100%. Consequently, the perspective that everyone can do well is not lost. If you don't have that kind of energy around as a reflection, you might have a tendency to get egotistical. Keeping a spiritual balance and outlook about your spiritual progress is difficult when that happens. You may find, also, that quite often the group energy stimulates your energy field and your accuracy as you explore your intuitive skills.

I have a group of friends around the country, and when we get together, we kid and joke with each other about our skills (or lack of them). We have a lot of fun and don't get overly serious except when it is appropriate to be serious. Something about group energy is very significant. Some people say they always do better with a group and that is often when they have no one with whom to share intuitive information. However, if you are in a group of like-minded people, the sense of safety is very meaningful. You can say almost anything, and others in the group are going to understand. Perhaps they are reading different books, and if you have had an experience you don't understand, others may be able to help you. Being part of a group is very important for personal growth.

Key Number Seven—Practice, Practice, Practice

The seventh key to unlocking your intuition has three parts to it—practice, practice, practice! Confidence will come with practice and feedback. Intuition is like other skills. Even though an artist has wonderful talent, certain amounts of training and practice are required to develop that talent. You wouldn't expect to take one or two tennis lessons and be an excellent player. Like any skill or talent, intuition takes practice and feedback to gain confidence.

Having been in a scientific laboratory where I had the opportunity to practice, receive immediate and extensive feedback, and thus gain confidence was fortunate for me. One of the things people ask is "How can I practice? I can't go up to strangers on the street and say let me give you a reading! Let me tune into you. I want to practice." Actually, all you need to do is let your friends know that you are studying intuition, and they will usually say something like this: "Well, I don't believe in this, but here . . . here's a photograph, or here's my watch, or tune into me, or tune into my daughter." Most will be more than willing to have you practice with them, and at the same time, you have the freedom to say "I'm just learning."

Practice with a situation in which you don't have an emotional investment. Take the newspaper, and with an election tomorrow (you don't care who wins) decide who is going to win. Keep in mind though that if you are a staunch party member, your conclusion might be colored. There are many TV shows (like a quiz show) you can practice with and get immediate feedback. After you have developed a track record and want to make decisions using your intuition (along with your intellect) about important issues in your life, you have confidence that you can be objective.

Here are other suggestions for practicing. When you are standing in front of an elevator, decide which of the elevators is going to come first. If you are shopping for a particular object, select three or four stores where you might find it; then intuit which store will have the object. Intuit the price as well. Then call the stores for confirmation. Is it the store you have intuited? Is the price higher or lower? If you want to play the stock market, pick a stock. Will it go higher or lower? What will the selling price be? While listening to the news, intuit outcomes, such as what the verdict is going to be in a trial which is in progress.

An example of this happened for me several years ago when Bruce Kimball, a diving champion, was trying out for the Olympic diving competition. Before the time for tryouts, he was driving drunk, drove down the street at eighty miles an hour with his headlights off, and crashed into a group of teenagers. He killed two of them. One of those killed was my brother's son. My brother desperately wanted to know: "Will he go to jail? Will he go trial? How many years will he get? How many will he serve?" He came to me and said, "I must know this information. I can't live with it if he isn't going to be punished in some way." I replied, "I don't see a trial, but I see Kimball getting seven years and serving five-and-a-half." "Well," he said, "it's not enough; but at least he will go to jail." A jury was picked, and on the day of the trial my brother said, "Well, so much for psychic ability."

The first person on the stand was the policewoman who arrived first at the scene. The prosecution had colored pictures of the victims to show to the jury along with a description from this police woman. Of course, Bruce Kimball's lawyer objected. Five minutes into the trial, the parties involved went in the judge's chamber and came out an hour later. Bruce Kimball pleaded "nolo contendere." The trial never happened. He was sentenced to seven years and served five-and-a-half. Because I had a big emotional investment in the outcome—it was my nephew and my brother—I had to get into that place inside myself where I knew I could be objective. With years of experience, I have confidence in my ability to be objective enough to do this type of reading.

Other circumstances in which you can practice using your intuition are in business situations to determine if a corporation is having financial difficulties or going to merge with another. Before the mail carrier arrives, decide what will show up in your mail box. Are there bills? Is it junk mail? How many pieces? Is the mail personal letters? If they are, do they contain happy news or sad? Is there anything out of the ordinary, such as notification that you are a winner in a million-dollar sweepstakes?

While driving to work, if you don't have an assigned parking place, decide where you will find one, which street will it be on, how far it will be from the office. Select one person in the office and decide what color he or she is going to wear. Is it a solid color or part of a print; is it dark or bright? Feel the mood of a particular person before you meet with him or her. Is the person happy or depressed? Is he or she pleased with work or looking for a change? This exercise can be used for social engagements also. An attorney can sense whether the client has all the necessary information or if he will have to spend many hours gathering information. Will the case have to be settled in court? Heard by a jury or a judge?

Are you a sales rep? How many sales were completed today, this week, this month? Of the people contacted today, which will buy now? Which will buy later? Which ones won't buy? In sports, whether you're a team player or a spectator, decide who will be the winner and by how many points.

Teachers can intuit which students in the class will excel, which ones will receive average grades, which ones will need the most help. Before giving a test, intuit the percentage of the ones that will pass. This may assist you in helping the right students before their problems cause them to lose interest and fail.

When the phone rings, ask yourself who is calling. Do you see yourself talking on the phone or do you see yourself handing the phone to someone else? Sense whether it is a man or a woman on the line. Is it an everyday type of call, just to talk? Or is it from someone you haven't expected to hear from? Is it a long distance or local call? If someone is expecting a baby, "see" the announcement. What is the due date? How much will the baby weigh? When will gold be X number of dollars, or when will it be ten dollars more than today? If you are expecting a letter or check, on which day of the week will it arrive?

What will be the temperature at this time tomorrow? Will the stock market rise or fall and by how many points . . . the headline in tomorrow's paper . . . the next person to make a comment about your appearance . . . the home mortgage rate . . . who is going to be on the next cover of *Time* magazine?

Remember that rehearsing with situations which are not emotional issues for you will allow you the practice and feedback important to monitoring your accuracy.

> **"Each one who has a soul**
> **has a psychic power."** 5392-1
> **Edgar Cayce**

4

Energy Sensing:
Hands as Sensory Systems

I remember from my high school science class learning about atoms and molecules—the unseen particles that make up the universe. It was a revelation to me to learn that the components of these particles are moving at unimaginable speeds, yet somehow still creating the illusion of solid matter. Even more astounding was the fact that there are vast amounts of space between these moving particles—*more space, in fact, than physical matter!* For the first time, I became aware (at least intellectually) that the walls, the desks, the chairs, and even my own body were really not solid objects at all.

That was years ago, and since then, our perceptions of the universe have changed incredibly. Today scientists no longer explain the universe simply in terms of atoms and molecules—instead the key word is energy.

Modern physicists tell us that the entire universe is really made up of matter and energy in constant motion. The "boundaries" we see between things or what we perceive as the real world is, in part, an illusion. Because, in reality, particles of everything in the universe, including you and me, flow into each other just as the air we breathe flows through each and every one of us.

Attempting to describe this energy in motion is as difficult as describing electricity. Although we all know what electricity does and the uses that it can be put to, few people can really tell what it is. Even scientists have difficulty describing it. Energy, like electricity, presents the same problem. We know that energy comprises the physical and non–physical universe, but this still does not explain what energy is. Fortunately, it is not necessary to know what energy is to be able to experience its activity.

In the 1960s Cleve Backster, polygraph expert and creator of the Backster Zone Comparison Test, conducted hundreds of experiments proving that plants, eggs, yogurt, lettuce leaves, and even bacteria respond to threats to their well-being! His book, *Primary Perception: Biocommunication with Plants, Living Foods, and Human Cells*, explains in detail the connection we have with everything and everyone!

During one of my business trips I was scheduled to take a plane from the Northeast to Orlando. When I arrived at the departure gate and saw the plane, I was suddenly hit with an overpowering sensation that felt like a wall. I sensed that there was something wrong with the plane and in an effort to discern the seriousness of the problem (and because I could not delay my Orlando arrival), I mentally scanned the airplane to ascertain whether it would arrive safely at its destination. After the scanning, I felt as though the plane and its passengers would arrive safely, and so I boarded in spite of the feeling that I had first experienced.

While in flight, the plane encountered a tremendous storm and was literally struck by lightning! There was a loud noise, the lights dimmed, and the plane suddenly dropped hundreds of feet in just a few moments. After a few minutes the plane seemed to become more stabilized, although it continued to wobble. Finally, the captain announced over the loudspeaker that the plane had been struck by lightning, that the windshield had shattered, and that the stabling rod was affected. Although he had requested permission to turn around and land in Atlanta, the control tower had encouraged his continuation to Orlando where they would prepare for an emergency landing. The plane wobbled for the duration of the trip, and thankfully it landed safely without any harm to its passengers or crew.

Although it may be difficult to explain how an experience such as this is even possible, we do know that energy fields emanate from everything: tables, chairs, plants, planes, animals, and people. An energy field is in constant motion and is something like the force field surrounding a bar magnet. It flows from every part of your body, and it is as much a part of you as your arms and legs. The purpose of energy sensing is to feel the different subtle energies emanating from you, other people, or even objects. When you begin to experience these energy fields for yourself, you will understand that they are as physical and real as your own body. You will find that everyone's energy field is unique and is influenced by the person's state of physical, mental, emotional, and spiritual health.

On one occasion, I was standing in an office speaking with a secretary when I again felt a "wall" bang into me. I turned to look and saw a little boy about six feet away who, I discovered, was autistic. To me, autism felt like a very rigid aura. Later, I discovered that this rigid "wall" allows only every third or fourth word to get through to the autistic individual. Is it any wonder that communication is so difficult? In another instance, during one of my ESP classes, I happened to be standing with my back to a student. Without even looking at the individual, I suddenly sensed that this person had a very powerful psychic potential. The aura felt energized. In time, my feeling proved accurate as the individual became a professional intuitive.

The energy around all people is somehow molded by their personal situation and current state of mind. Although you will probably have your own sense of how different emotions feel in my own experience, the energy from individuals who are depressed feels slow and heavy. Encountering this energy is almost like the feeling one encounters when walking through deep water. Conversely, the energy from someone who is happy feels light and bouncy, almost tingly or charged with an electrical feeling. Anger feels like sharp points or darts. Serenity feels smooth, even and soft. Frustration feels very tangled. All emotions have their own "feelings" and effect upon the energy field. In time and with experience, you will be able to describe for yourself how one person's energy field seems different from another's, and you will be able to interpret how this *feeling* is connected to the individual's emotional and personal situation.

Although energy is emanating from all parts of the body, the areas where the energy field is most intense are the hands, feet, solar plexus (navel area), and the top of the head. One of the easiest energy–sensing exercises you can experience concentrates only upon the hands. Using your hands as sensory systems, you may feel such things as heat, coolness, or even magnetic sensations coming from another individual. As you practice, you may immediately begin to notice differences of frequency in the energy and perhaps even have distinct impressions of what those frequencies mean. It is a good place to start sensitizing yourself to energy fields and to ESP.

Here are some things to keep in mind as you prepare for any energy sensing exercise:

Step One: *Relax and concentrate.* Without a relaxed state of body and mind, it is unlikely that you will achieve the sensitivity necessary to experience the full benefits of your intuitive processes. Begin this exercise (and every intuitive activity) with time for relaxation.

Step Two: *Concentration comes next.* Begin by putting your complete attention into your hands. Wherever you focus your attention is where you will receive your impressions. With keen, one–pointed focused attention, you will become sensitized to all the subtle feelings coming through your hands. In fact, your hands can be compared to some of the most sensitive instruments in the world and can work as your very own radar. If your attention wanders, gently bring it back to your point of focus. With practice, the experience will seem more natural, and you will get much better at doing it.

Step Three: *Simply experience the subtle vibrations and sensations before attempting to analyze them.* This experience is not so much an exercise of the intellect as it is an exercise of your feelings. Your intellect may try to talk you out of the experience with thoughts such as "I'm no good at this." "I'm just not psychic." "This must not be right because it's different from what I expected." "I don't feel anything." "This is just my imagination." Conversely, if you bring a relaxed state of body and mind to the exercise with an attitude such as "I am not really concerned if I do well or not, I just want to try it," it is much easier for you to relax into the experience. Sometimes it is best to take a childlike attitude, one full of enthusiasm for the experience itself. Do not be concerned about failing or measuring up to someone else's performance. A child is naturally spontaneous and eager to participate in an experience on a feeling level. If you can recapture this attitude, the exercise becomes easier and you will have greater success with it. Rather than talking yourself out of your experience, let yourself have fun with it. See where it takes you.

Step Four: *After fully experiencing the sensations and feelings, there will come a time for the intellect to play its role.* At that point you can ask yourself: "What do I feel and where do I feel it?" Analyze the sensations you pick up from your partner's hands. What sensations are there? Are you sensing it through the fingertips, the palms, or somewhere else? Adults often analyze too quickly, halting the experience before allowing themselves ample time to explore their sensations. If you find that you are analyzing too quickly, simply move the intellect gently aside with your mind and put your keen, one-pointed attention back into your hands.

Step Five: *At the end of each experience, you should take time to verbalize or to note your impressions.* Keeping a journal helps you to discover greater depths of information as you learn. For example, you may wish to draw a picture of your hands and the sensations that seemed to surround them. Communicate whatever you sensed, felt, or experienced, as well as where you experienced it. Avoid any interpretations at this point. Do not try to guess what your sensations and your feelings mean because this will only confuse the learning process. You will find that as you develop these abilities, you will intuitively make connections between the feelings and what the feelings mean. For now, simply communicate your impressions as completely and accurately as you can, because it will help you learn how the ESP process works for you.

> **"Our past lies embedded within us written**
> **in the language of the nervous system."**
> **Eric Kandel**
> **Howard Hughes Medical Institute at Columbia University**

EXERCISES

Energy-Sensing Exercises
(For individuals)

The next two exercises are important because they will give you your first experiences with sensing the energies that emanate from different parts of your body. Only as you start to sense the way these energies feel will you begin to gain the experience you need in order to interpret what specific feelings may mean.

Exercise One

Sit comfortably with your feet flat on the floor and your hands in your lap. Very gently tell yourself to relax. Put your keen, one–pointed attention into your hands and be aware of the energy radiating from them.

Hold your hands in front of you with your palms facing together in a hand clapping position, keeping your palms about two inches apart. Attune your awareness to the subtle vibrations of your energy field between your hands . . . Perhaps you feel warmth or the movement of air or an invisible pressure . . . Whatever it is, become aware of it . . .

Bring your hands together so that they nearly touch. Then, slowly move them apart. Notice at what point you no longer feel the energy field . . . Notice at what point you're most aware of it . . .

Try this exercise with your eyes open, and then a second time with your eyes closed; see if there are any noticeable differences in your concentration or in your sensing ability.

Exercise Two

Sit comfortably, and very gently tell yourself to relax. Put your keen, one–pointed attention into the outer layer of your skin . . . Visualize the energy field surrounding you. Feel the energy radiating from every pore . . .

Choose a part of your body that you know is healthy, and place your hand about two inches from this spot. It could be your shoulder, your upper leg, your ear, your chest, your left foot—any part of your body that you know is in perfect health. Now, put your keen, one–pointed attention into your hand and be aware of the energy emanating from that healthy part of your body . . .

Note how the energy feels . . . Bring your hand close to the spot until it almost touches . . . Then, slowly move your hand away . . . Notice at what point you no longer feel the energy field . . . Notice at what point you're most aware of it . . . Make a note of your impressions . . .

Now, choose a part of your body that is in poor health or one that was once damaged or injured at some time in your life. Place your hand about two inches from that spot. Put your keen, one–pointed attention into your hand and be aware of how the energy feels to you . . . Does this energy feel different from that of the perfectly healthy area? If so, how is the energy different? . . . Become aware of your impressions . . . and note them . . .

Repeat this exercise several times, focusing and refocusing your attention from the healthy to the unhealthy (or once injured) areas. Become aware of any differences you feel in the energy . . .

If you have any areas in your body which are in pain, you may wish to move ahead to the "Healing Exercise" described in the *Healing* chapter of this book.

Exercise Three
(For this exercise, you will need a deck of playing cards.)

This exercise is more than just a game, for it will allow you to begin fine-tuning the sensitivity of your hand. This increased sensitivity can be put to very practical uses in both your business and personal life. For example, with practice and in time you may be able to scan the yellow pages and "sense" which realtor to use, which doctor would be best for your child, which customer will make the most productive business contact, etc.

First Variation: Remove two cards from the deck, one black and one red, and lay them face up on the table. At first, use two face cards *or* two numbered cards, but not a combination of both face and number cards.

Sit comfortably and very gently tell yourself to relax. Put your keen, one–pointed attention into your hands. Using the right or left hand, scan both cards—face up, one at a time. Try the exercise with your left hand, and then try it with your right hand. See if one of your hands appears to be more sensitive than the other . . . If so, which one?

Become aware of any differences you feel between the red and the black cards . . . You may notice that one card feels warmer or cooler, harder or softer, or stickier or smoother than the other. These are very subjective terms for an experience that you will become aware of and will have to describe in your own way . . . Note the different sensations between red and black . . .

When you have a sense of the difference between the red and black cards, it's time to begin. Turn the cards over, shuffle them, and lay the deck face down on the table. Scan the cards one at a time, seeing how well you can separate the red from the black . . .

(Note: you have a 50–50 chance of picking the right color each time at random; see how well you do with scanning on a run through the entire deck of fifty-two cards.)

Second Variation: Shuffle the deck thoroughly; then place the deck face down on the table. Take one card at a time from the top of the deck and place it face down on the table in front of you. Scan the card as before . . . If you sense it is a red card, put it in one pile, and if it's black, put it in another . . . Continue scanning one card at a time until you have scanned every card in the deck. Keep all the cards face down until you are done . . .

When you've finished, you will have two piles, one for the red cards and one for the black. Gather the red pile and count the number of red cards you find there. Next, gather the black pile and then count the number of black cards. These are all of your correct answers. The combined total is your score for that round. Repeat the exercise to see if you can increase your score. (Of course, a perfect score is fifty-two!)

Energy-Sensing Exercise
(For groups of two or more)

This exercise explores the energy field of another person and gives you an experience in discerning the subtle differences of another individual's energy—his or her moods, feelings, perhaps even a quality you may sense about him or her. In "real-life," you may use a similar technique to discover what a child needs, how to approach a supervisor, or what an individual is really feeling, regardless of what he or she may be saying.

First Variation: Choose a partner and sit comfortably, facing that person. Sit fairly close so that your knees are almost touching. Relax and concentrate. You may both wish to do a relaxation exercise before proceeding any further . . .

When you are ready, put your keen, one-pointed attention into your hands and become aware of the energy field surrounding and radiating from them . . . Next, position your hands as follows: one partner with the palms of both hands facing up, the other with both palms facing down and directly over the partner's hands. There should be about two to four inches between you and your partner's hands.

Slowly, feel the energy field surrounding and radiating from your partner's hands . . . Give yourself time to experience the subtle energy . . . When you are ready, ask yourself "What am I feeling and where am I feeling it?" . . . Share this information with your partner . . .

When you have explored this exercise and your impressions for five to ten minutes, change positions with your partner and allow his or her hands to be palm down over yours. Just as you did, let your partner slowly feel the energy field surrounding and radiating from your hands . . . Have your partner describe what he or she is feeling and where the feeling is.

When both of you have explored this portion of the exercise, place your hands back over your partner's . . . After focusing your keen, one-pointed attention in your hands, slowly raise your hands up and away from your partner's and feel the change in the energy field . . . At what point are you no longer aware of the energy field emanating from your partner's hands? . . . At what point are you most aware of it? . . . Move your hands up and down several times to become aware of these changes and to confirm them. Ask yourself "What am I feeling and where am I feeling it?" . . . Share this information with your partner. Then, switch roles and let your partner repeat this process . . .

For this exercise, you may wish to switch with other partners several times in order to sense the many variations in another individual's energy field and your own sensitivities.

Change partners again and sit comfortably. To the partner whose hands are on top, move your hands in a circular motion over your partner's hands . . . Ask yourself "What am I feeling and where am I feeling it?" Share this information with your partner. Then, switch roles and repeat the process.

Second Variation: Change partners and sit comfortably. In this step, one partner will use a visualization and concentration technique to raise the temperature of one hand. The other partner, applying the same energy–sensing techniques used previously, will identify the "hot" hand. Decide between the two of you who will be the first to raise his or her hand temperature, and who will be the first to sense it.

When you are ready, sit comfortably, close your eyes, and very gently tell yourself to relax . . .

For the individual who is raising the temperature of one hand, place your hands on your lap with the palms facing up. Make a mental decision which hand you are going to make hot, but don't tell your partner. Now, put your keen, one–pointed attention into that hand . . . Feel the energy radiating from it. Visualize and feel this hand becoming very hot . . . You are altering the temperature of your hand with your mind, knowing that the body follows the commands of the mind . . .

Visualize and feel your hand radiating an intense heat . . . You could also imagine holding your hand in the sunshine, or near a fire, or immersed in hot water. Concentrate on raising the temperature of your hand until you feel the heat radiating from it . . . Let your partner know when you are ready . . .

For the individual who is planning to identify the "hot" hand, maintain a relaxed state of body and mind, and put your keen, one–pointed attention into your hands. When your partner is ready, place your hands palms down, about two to four inches above your partner's hands . . . Become aware of any subtle differences in the energy field . . . Does one hand feel different from the other? . . . Where does it feel different? . . . Some people experience this as an increase in heat, others as an increase in pressure. . . . When you are ready, tell your partner which hand you sense is the hot hand, and tell your partner how you made this choice.

When you have finished, switch roles and repeat the experience . . .

Finally, allow plenty of time to regroup and for everyone to discuss his or her individual experiences. (Interestingly enough, science has shown that by raising the temperature of one's hand, an individual can help prevent or stop migraine headaches or even deal with chronic pain, making this exercise both practical and simple.)

Energy-Sensing Exercise
(For groups of five or more)

This can be an important exercise for increasing your sensitivity to the energy of a group. In addition, it also can be effective for building community and teamwork as individuals are often bonded by this experience with one another.

This is a good way to begin or to end group sessions that explore intuition. To get started, have your group form a circle. If possible, alternate with men and women around the circle, balancing the male/ female energy as much as possible. Once the circle is formed, hold hands with your partners on either side. Every participant is to follow the instructions simultaneously.

First, close your eyes and take a deep breath . . . Very gently tell yourself to relax, knowing that the body follows the commands of the mind . . .

Next, take your keen, one-pointed attention and put it into the outer layer of your skin. Visualize or feel the energy field radiating from your body . . . At first, you may think you are only imagining your energy field, but know it is really there . . . Let yourself visualize it . . . Feel the energy flowing around your body . . . And now, because you are standing together in a circle, your energy fields are beginning to blend together, forming a group energy field . . . With your mind, or your imagination, expand your awareness and experience this group energy . . . Take time to feel the energy of the circle . . .

Now, in your imagination, visualize the face of someone for whom you have great love and affection . . . Experience that love and affection . . . When you feel it, take the feeling of that thought and emotion and direct it around the circle to your right . . . Maintain a very relaxed state of body and mind, and feel the change in the energy as it moves through you and around the circle . . . Give yourself some time to experience this fully . . .

One at a time, volunteer to take turns standing in the center of the circle and feel the energy directed toward you . . . Have the volunteer enter the circle and stand comfortably with eyes closed and arms at the sides . . . (If the individual is not known to the group, have the person state his or her name once inside the circle.)

Have the group members keep their eyes closed and take the thought and feeling of love and healing and direct it toward the person in the center of the circle, thinking the individual's name with keen, one-pointed attention . . . Focus for thirty to forty-five seconds before moving onto the next individual, repeating for as many volunteers as would like to take a turn standing in the circle . . .

When everyone has finished, have each individual share with the group what he or she experienced . . . Where did you feel the energy? . . . What was it like? . . . How did you feel as both a member of the entire group and as the person in the center of the circle? . . .

Repeat this experience as often as you like.

PROCESSING
Energy Sensing

Process what happened with this technique. What did you experience? What caught your attention?

What worked? What energized you? What were the low points? What frustrated you?

What has been your most significant learning? What are the implications of this learning?

What are some of the ways you could use this technique in your life?

5

Scanning Energy Fields or Auras

A ura or energy-field scanning is simply an extension of working with energy sensing. It is a fairly simple technique to learn as well as one of the most versatile and useful of intuitive skills. In energy sensing, remember your focus was to feel the energy field around your partner's hands. The aura-scanning exercise is similar to this, but instead of feeling the energy from your partner's hands, you will be sensing the energy emanating from every part of the body. In other words, you will be using your hand as a scanning device to sense the subtle differences in your partner's aura or energy field.

There are many practical uses for aura scanning. You can use it to discern health issues, find lost objects, and even locate missing persons. A number of years ago I was working with the police to find the body of a man who had been missing for several days. He was last seen on his boat on the Niagara River near Buffalo, New York. The police felt certain that the man had fallen overboard and drowned, but up to that point divers had been unable to locate the body. I laid out a map of the area where he had disappeared and began scanning it slowly. With my keen, one-pointed attention in my hand, I concentrated upon only one thing: finding the man's body.

As I scanned the map, I was suddenly aware of a different sensation at one point in the river—to me, it felt like a slight resistance on the map. The rest of the map felt smooth. In my own experience, I have come to discover that while using this technique when something is not the answer, it is smooth. The area of the resistance appeared to be a place in the river quite a distance from the spot where the man's boat was found. I scanned this area of the map again and again, just to verify that I had pinpointed the location. Each time, the same area felt different from the rest of the map. I reported my findings. Later, police divers found the body at the exact location I had pointed out.

Most people will never have to work with the police to recover a missing body; however, this is the very same technique you can use to find a misplaced valuable, such as a ring, a watch, or a wallet. If you lose an object, it is fairly easy to use aura scanning for yourself. For years I have used this technique, and it has saved a lot of time and worry. The procedure is simple. Instead of a map, just make a quick sketch of the area where you believe the item was lost and then proceed to use the scanning technique.

For example, if an object was lost somewhere in your home, draw a simple floor plan that contains the rooms in your house (if the original plans for the house are on hand, you can use them instead). You may wish to draw larger pieces of furniture, such as your couch, the bed, the dresser, etc. Once the sketch of your home is complete, take the time to do a simple relaxation exercise. Once you feel relaxed, focus your keen, one-pointed attention onto your hands, visualize the object in your mind, and then scan the map until you feel a difference of some kind. This may have to do with warmth or coolness, the sensations of fullness versus emptiness, or even a sense of "knowing." The feelings you have will depend upon your own sensory processes. Throughout the exercise you should be relaxed, concentrating upon only one thing: locating the lost object. As with everything else, practice will allow the process to become easier.

By now, you should have practiced the energy-sensing technique described in the last chapter. You should have also experienced the exercise with several partners, becoming aware of the differences in energy from one partner to another. One partner's energy might have felt tingly; perhaps the next was magnetic, or hot, or cooler, and so forth.

Now you are going to attempt to experience the differences in your partner's aura as you scan his or her body from head to foot. Your only objective is to find areas of the body where the energy feels different.

What kind of differences? Again, think back to your experiences with the energy sensing exercise. The first time you tried it you felt one sensation; when you changed partners, you probably felt something different. How did the energy radiating from the hands of your first partner feel different from the energy of your second, third, or fourth partners? These subtle differences in energy are also present throughout one individual's aura as well.

As you scan your partner's aura, one part of the body will feel noticeably different from another. One area may feel as if it has more pressure or it might feel cooler, or perhaps it will "feel" weaker. The reason is simply because energy radiating from a healthy part of the body can feel very smooth and even. However, unhealthy areas or areas that were once injured, radiate a different kind of energy, and you will be able to sense these areas because you will feel a difference of some kind: heat, cold, tingling, agitation, bulges or breaks, or some other sensation.

I learned the difference between "healthy" and "unhealthy" energy many years ago when I was working with a group of medical people. One was a chiropractor; and since I had never been to a chiropractor at that time, I asked him about his field and how it worked. He explained to me how manipulation techniques were used to adjust the spine, neck, and other parts of the body. Essentially, these adjustments opened up the body's energy pathways—chiropractors describe it as nerve functions. As a result, patients are relieved of aches, pains, and other physical problems.

He asked me if I wanted to scan the aura of one of his patients before he made the adjustment. "Maybe you can tell me where this man needs his treatment," he said. I agreed and began to scan the man's entire energy field, concentrating on finding the differences. As I scanned his back, I felt a sudden, noticeable difference in the area of the lower back. The energy felt aggravated, as though there was too much energy in that spot. The chiropractor verified that was the area needing treatment.

After the adjustments had been made, he asked me if I wanted to scan the area again to see if I could detect any change. I expected to feel even more energy radiating from that area of his back, but instead the energy field felt smooth and evened out all over. The treatment had relieved the aggravation, and his energy field reflected the change in his condition.

At this point, you may be asking yourself this question: "If I find a difference in an individual's aura, does that mean the person has a serious problem?" Usually, this is not the case. There are all sorts of conditions that may show up as differences in the energy field. A health problem from the past is one example. Suppose you broke your leg many years ago. You probably walked around in a cast for a month or two, and in time, the leg healed and the cast came off. As far as you are concerned, your leg is as good as new. But wherever there has been a change in the physical body, there will be a detectable change in the energy field. Even though your leg has completely healed and you may no longer think about the fact that it was once broken, the bone has been permanently changed, and this change will be evident in the aura.

What will this difference feel like? If five people scanned the leg, all five might describe the experience in a different way. One might say it feels cold; another might describe it as being agitated, and still another might sense a break in the energy field. It really does not matter what label you put on the experience; what matters is that you are able to sense the difference in the aura in your own way. With practice, you will be able to combine aura scanning with other intuitive techniques so that when you detect a difference, you will be able to discover what the problem is, and whether it is in the past or the present. For now, the important thing is to simply experience the differences in the energy field.

We have seen that a past problem such as a broken leg can show up in the present as a difference in the aura. Therefore, there is absolutely no reason to believe that every difference you feel points to a serious health problem. It can be almost anything, either minor or serious, and it can be from the past, present, or future. For example, if you notice a difference around the heart area, it could be that your partner needs to change something about his or her lifestyle in order to prevent a heart attack. It might be that your partner suffered a minor heart attack many years ago. It could suggest that your partner is emotionally closed, or perhaps the fact is that your partner suffers from heartburn. Only experience and the utilization of additional intuitive skills will enable you to discern the appropriate interpretation.

You may also pick up temporary problems. If something you had for lunch upset your stomach, it could show up as a difference in the energy field near the abdomen. Chronic problems such as a sinus condition or ulcers will be noticeable even if the condition is not bothering the individual at the moment. You may pick up sympathetic problems in the body as well. For example, someone with a pinched nerve in the spine may have problems with muscles or organs in other parts of the body as a result. The individual may not be consciously aware of these problems, but they can show up as differences in the energy field nonetheless.

As you scan the aura, take a lighthearted, receptive attitude. Play at it rather than work at it. After all, what difference does it make if you are right or wrong? This is not a contest or an exam.

Whenever you pick up a difference in your partner's aura, begin by locating the area; pinpoint the area if you can. Then get a good sense of what it is you are feeling. Does it feel hot, cold, energized, agitated, or magnetic? Does it feel like a break or a bulge in the energy field? Ask yourself: "What am I feeling and where am I feeling it?" When you have answered these questions for yourself, tell your partner what you are sensing. Your partner's feedback should be as complete as possible because this is the most important part of the exercise.

Both you and your partner have active roles to play. As your partner scans your aura, listen carefully to what he or she is telling you and stop to think before responding. Remember that your partner could be picking up a minor problem that you have not thought about in years. If you cannot recall a problem, tell your partner there is nothing that comes to mind. Also be sure to let your partner know when he or she is accurate. Offer your partner as much feedback as you can.

What happens if you scan your partner's aura and do not pick up any differences at all, even after scanning the aura from head to toe? There are two possibilities: either your partner is in perfect health, or you are too tense or too unfocused to pick up the differences. There is a remote possibility that your partner has no weak spots in the entire body, but it is much more likely that you need to relax and concentrate.

Relaxation comes first. Remember the playful, childlike attitude? Then concentrate on what you want to know—you are simply looking for differences in the energy field.

EXERCISES

Aura-Scanning Exercise
(For groups of two or more)

This exercise will allow you to discern the different energy sensations surrounding an individual. These different energies may indicate areas where there are (or where there have been) changes or problems in the physical body. For example, the energy surrounding healthy areas may feel smooth or warm while an area where a bone was once broken may feel fractured, cold, or uneven. This exercise simply gives you additional experience sensing subtle energies.

After reading and discussing the material in this chapter, choose a partner; it is preferable to choose someone you do not know. Face your partner, standing comfortably with your feet spread slightly and your arms at your sides. If necessary, this exercise can be done with one or both of you sitting. Another option is to have the individual being scanned lie on a table or the floor—which is really the ideal position for scanning the aura, if there's space. For this exercise, have the person being scanned remove his or her shoes, since you'll be scanning the feet as well. Find a place in the room that gives you and your partner plenty of space. Decide who will be first to scan the aura . . .

For the individual being scanned, simply relax and focus your attention inward throughout the experience. When your partner begins to tell you of his or her impressions for feedback, don't respond too quickly. Take time to think of present and past conditions, even very minor ones.

For the individual doing the aura scanning, take a few moments to become relaxed . . . When you've achieved a sense of relaxation, focus your keen, one-pointed attention into your hands . . . Concentrate on your intent: "I am scanning the aura for differences in the energy field." Make your scanning movements slow and deliberate. If you scan too quickly, you will miss the subtle differences. When you're ready, it's time to begin scanning your partner's aura, beginning with the head.

Get a sense of the intensity and the width of your partner's energy field by bringing the palm of your hand slowly toward the side of your partner's head. Use the hand you feel most comfortable using. Move your hand about two feet from the head or shoulder area, and then slowly bring it in toward the body until you can feel the energy field. Move your hand in and out of the energy field in order to familiarize yourself with the vibration . . . At no time should your hand actually touch your partner's body . . .

Now, begin scanning your partner's aura. Using one hand, scan the entire aura from the head to the toes. Slowly, beginning at the top of the head, scan the sides and back of the head, then the face . . . Scan under the chin and across the throat and neck area . . . Ask your partner to move one arm to the side and scan along the top of the arm from the shoulder to the hand.

Work carefully over your partner's hand, scanning each finger separately . . . Move your hand along the underside of your partner's arms beginning at the tips of the fingers to the armpit . . . Repeat the sequence on both of your partner's arms. Have your partner lift both arms and scan across the torso from side to side . . . (If your partner is lying down, scan your partner's chest and then have him or her roll over as you scan the back.) Scan the legs, one at a time, from the hips to the feet . . . Scan each toe individually . . . Then have your partner turn around and scan the back of the legs from the buttocks to the heels. Finally, scan across the entire back from side to side . . .

Maintain a relaxed and concentrated state of body and mind as you scan your partner's aura. Remember that your objective is to find the areas where the aura feels different . . . When you are aware of an area that feels different, ask yourself: "What am I feeling and where am I feeling it?" Move your hand slowly back and forth over this area until you are quite clear of its source. Then communicate what you feel to your partner . . .

When the person scanning your aura tells you of a change, think carefully before responding. Your partner may be picking up a condition from the past that is no longer a concern to you, or a minor or temporary condition that you are not aware of . . .

If you find that you are distracted by watching your hand or looking at your partner as you scan the aura, try closing your eyes or pick out a spot on the floor or the wall to look at . . .

Above all, relax and have fun with this exercise. The more relaxed you are, the better you'll do with aura scanning.

When you have finished scanning your partner's aura, switch roles with this person and repeat the technique. You may also want to change partners and repeat the exercise . . .

When everyone has completed the exercise, regroup for a discussion of your experiences . . .

You may want to begin keeping a notebook of the physical sensations you have experienced and how this corresponded to your partner's feedback. The notes can be useful for future reference, helping you identify similar conditions in others.

Aura-Scanning Exercise
(For individuals)

The outcome of an intuitive experience is greatly affected by one's overall intent. Therefore, whatever one focuses upon with his or her keen, one-pointed attention will determine what types of sensations or feelings he or she has during the experience. The next two exercises will give you firsthand experience with attempting to sense the subtle variations in a map or a sketch while holding a particular intent in mind. In fact, this is one of the most practical intuitive exercises you can use in order to find a lost object or to discover more about a location before you even get there.

Exercise One

For this exercise, have a friend or someone in your family hide one of your valuables in the house, such as your car keys or wallet.

When that's been accomplished, simply sketch out a map containing a simple floor plan of your house . . . Be sure to draw larger objects or pieces of furniture (such as your couch, the bed, the dresser, etc.) Once the sketch of your home is complete, take time to do the simple relaxation exercise . . .

Sit comfortably with your feet flat on the floor and your hands in your lap. Very gently tell yourself to relax. Put your keen, one-pointed attention into your hands and become aware of the energy radiating through them . . .

Next, visualize the object in your mind, and tell yourself your objective is to find it. When you're ready, scan the floor plan until you feel a difference of some kind . . . Go over each room of your home until you can discern between the variations in energy . . .

When you've decided upon the room, see if you can hone in even closer and discover exactly where the object is . . . Tell your friend or family member your impressions, and get his or her feedback . . .

At first, you may only be able to discern the general location of the object, or the room it is in. Yet, with practice, you should be able to become much more skilled at the technique.

Exercise Two

Get a street map of an area or a neighborhood where you have never been and that is within driving distance. After becoming relaxed and focusing your keen, one-pointed attention into your hands, scan the map with the objective of feeling what is on a particular street. Try to feel through your hands how the houses look . . . What is unique about the area? . . . Are there gas stations or restaurants nearby or trees, parks, schools? Is it a peaceful and safe area? What about shopping areas? . . .

Record all of your impressions, giving yourself at least fifteen to twenty minutes to do a thorough job . . .

When you've finished, journey to the area and make note of the differences and similarities between what you felt and what was actually there.

MAPPING BIO-PLASMIC FIELDS

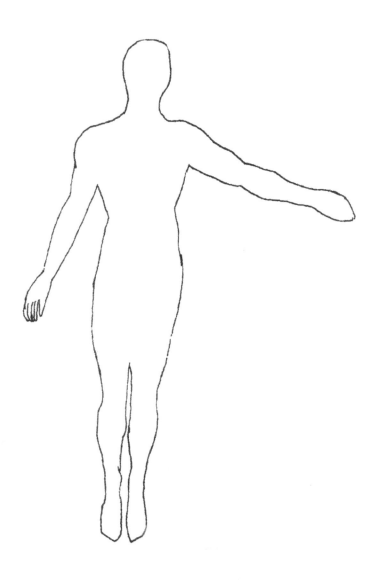

PROCESSING
Aura Scanning Technique

Process what happened with this technique. What did you experience? What caught your attention?

What worked? What energized you? What were the low points? What frustrated you?

What has been your most significant learning? What are the implications of this learning?

What are some of the ways you could use this technique in your life?

6

Aura Seeing

Most people believe everyone ends with his or her skin; however, there are some who can see or feel the energy surrounding the physical body. This energy field has been referred to as a(n):

- Aura
- Beta body
- Second body
- Halo
- Bio-plasmic field
- Morphogenic field
- Subtle body
- Astral body
- Pre-physical

But to paraphrase William Shakespeare "a rose by any other name is still a rose." Use the label that is comfortable for you.

The aura has:

- Multi-layers

- Multi-colors
- Multi-widths

Although the energy field appears to radiate from the body, in reality the body radiates from the various layers of the aura! These layers are said to be seven in number, multicolored, undulating, and constantly changing. Depending upon which books you read, different labels have been used to designate the layers. For purposes of simplicity, let's call the layers 1–7, starting with the layer farthest away from the body being #1. This layer, I believe, is our connection to that which has been called God, Higher Consciousness, Universal Intelligence, etc. When there is an imbalance in the spiritual, mental, emotional, or casual layer of the aura, this imbalance radiates down through the various layers of the aura to the physical body. It then manifests as physical problems, although the "problem" originated in one of the layers of the aura. Kirlian photography, pictures of the human aura, has shown images of illness appearing in the aura before manifesting in the physical body. Many books, articles, and papers have been written about diagnoses being done from Kirlian photos.

Seeing the aura . . .

The first time I thought I might be seeing auras was when I joined the Human Dimensions Institute in Buffalo, New York. I was twenty–nine at the time and had just begun a rigorous psychic development program. I had also started to get involved with meditation.

The auras I first saw looked like hazy clouds that appeared when I focused my eyes in a certain manner. However, this haziness did not appear just around people; I also saw it around plants, animals, tables, or anything else I looked at. At the time I had never even heard of auras appearing around objects like tables and chairs.

Because this was all very new to me, I eventually became concerned that there was something seriously wrong with my eyes and that I was not seeing auras at all. I had heard that the symptoms of glaucoma were hazy vision and shadows appearing around objects in a person's field of vision. Since this very closely described what I was experiencing, I became convinced that I had glaucoma. A visit to the ophthalmologist discounted my fears for there was no evidence of glaucoma. The oph-thalmologist told me that my eyes were in perfect condition.

Even though I did not have glaucoma, for a long time after that I was still skeptical about whether or not I was actually seeing auras. In time, I began testing my experiences in a very pragmatic manner. Whenever the opportunity arose during a reading and I saw what I thought might be an aura, I would ask questions related to what I was seeing. For example, if I saw dull gray spots around the heart area, I would ask the individual whether or not he or she had any heart problems. Often times I would find that these were the very individuals who had suffered heart attacks or in fact, had other problems with their hearts. These questions led me to the discovery that whenever the individual had physical or emotional problems, the aura itself appeared dull, gray, or perhaps darker around the affected areas of the body.

An individual's aura changes as his or her physical health or vitality changes. You may see breaks or bulges around the areas where there are physical problems. Emotional or mental states also show up in the aura, so if a person is depressed, angry, or troubled, his or her aura will reflect those emotions. For example, it may appear smaller or cloudier than normal, or the colors may be less intense. Someone who is feeling angry may have dark red spots in his or her energy field around the head or throat, but these spots may disappear when the anger subsides. From one person to the next, the aura appears different in size, shape, intensity, clarity, and brightness. Even the colors of the aura will appear different.

The aura contains the frequency of who we are physically, mentally, emotionally, and spiritually as well as the frequencies of all our past experiences, including past lives, and the energies of the decisions we have made consciously and unconsciously.

Although the aura appears to radiate from the body; in reality, our physical body is the result of the radiation inward.

Different books describing the aura will label the seven layers of the aura many ways, i.e. etheric double, causal, etc. I prefer to refer to these layers as 1, 2, 3, 4, 5, 6, and 7. The first level of the aura would be the farthest from the body with the seventh layer appearing to be closest to the physical body. In my opinion, this seventh layer is the energy that holds the moving molecules of our physical body together, thus appearing as a solid form with energy radiating from it, when the opposite is true.

The layers of the aura extend out from the body to a distance of several feet or more. There are many different perspectives on just how many layers or levels there are. Some say there are two to three layers; others say there are seven or more. The only point of agreement is that there is much more to learn about energy fields. Right now, the important thing is to experience seeing the aura for yourself and through practice and persistence, discover what the appearance of the aura means to you personally.

Seeing energy fields or auras is really not that difficult; in fact, it is simply a process of learning to "see" in a new way. Trying too hard will only prevent you from seeing them at all. Rather than striving to see the aura, let it appear to you. It is not so much an active "looking" as it is a passive "seeing." This is something of a paradox: if you try to see it, you probably won't, and if you look directly at the aura, it may disappear.

At first, you may perceive the aura as a haze, glow, whiteness, or cloudiness around the head and shoulders, or simply as an intensification of the background color around the individual. This thin, silvery haze outlining the body is, in fact, the etheric double. Seeing the aura for the first time can be quite a surprise, and there are many different reactions to this experience. Some think it is their eyes playing tricks on them. Others think they are imagining things or seeing an optical illusion, an after image, or a shadow caused by the lights in the room. People who wear glasses begin wondering if it is time to get their prescriptions checked. Some think they have suddenly developed double vision. The aura is real; moreover, it is not an illusion or simply a figment of the imagination.

Sometimes, there are individuals who can see the colors of the aura immediately, appearing as a shimmering, pulsating field around the body. The colors of the aura are not quite like the colors you are used to seeing. These are finer, more subtle colors, and the colors will vary depending upon the individual's physical, mental, emotional, and spiritual condition. For most people, seeing the colors of the aura takes practice and persistence.

If you are having trouble seeing the aura, there are usually three stumbling blocks that can account for it: the intellect, past conditioning, and tension. Although the intellect is important to the intuitive process, the logical mind cannot experience ESP or see auras; it can only sort out the experiences once they have occurred. When the intellect acts as a stumbling block, you will hear yourself saying things like: "It must be my imagination." "My eyes are playing tricks on me." "I'm probably just seeing a shadow or a reflection." "It's only an optical illusion." "There must be something on my glasses." These are all some of the common responses of the intellect to this experience. Of course, a healthy skepticism can be a good thing, but the important thing to remember about the intellect is that it only accepts experiences that are familiar and can be logically explained.

The second stumbling block is past conditioning. Much of what we call logic is really conditioning. As much as we pride ourselves on thinking for ourselves and being open to new experiences, many of us are not. For the most part, we believe what we have been taught to believe. And most of us are very aware of the fact that our school system, those who were in authority in our lives, and even our religious backgrounds probably did not tell us about seeing auras. It has not been part of the mainstream world view of how things are supposed to be. The only way to deal with this bias is to allow yourself to recognize that no one possesses all the answers or understands all the mysteries of life. Learn to put your past conditioning and your intellect aside for a time. The intellect will have the opportunity to analyze your experience later.

For many of us, however, the biggest stumbling block to seeing an aura is the third problem of tension. In fact, tension in any form keeps us from experiencing ESP. As you practice relaxation and learn to do it at the command of your will, seeing the aura can become an easy, almost effortless experience. Trying too hard to develop your intuitive abilities will generally keep you from having a positive experience or from doing very well.

In time, as you develop your abilities, you will begin seeing more and more colors in the aura. The colors of the aura can be interpreted, although the specific meaning often differs depending upon who is doing the interpreting. Most individuals who have worked with color interpretation do agree on the basic principles. To help you with these principles, the list that follows offers a brief interpretation taken from my own experience. Although it generally agrees with most individuals' experiences, as always, the best way to learn interpretation is to work with your own practice and experience

Red
Red is the first primary color and traditionally has represented the physical world. It is the color of strength and vitality. Red indicates a strong-minded individual, a materialistic outlook on life, and often a warm and affectionate nature. Red also represents the power of the deepest human passions: courage, love, hate, anger, sex, and vengeance. Very dark red indicates a tendency to selfishness. Cloudy red indicates greed or cruelty. Bright, clear red can indicate generosity, praiseworthy ambition, and a strong, commanding, magnetic personality.

Pink
Pink indicates a quiet, refined, and modest individual with a love of artistic surroundings and beauty in all forms. It can indicate lasting devotion and self-sacrifice.

Orange
Orange is the color of life's vital forces and the energy of the sun. It can indicate a well-balanced individual who is active, vital, and energetic. Orange is expressive of wisdom and good-reasoning abilities. People in responsible positions who would rather rule than serve often have orange in their auras. They are usually tactful in managing others and get along well with people.

Yellow
Yellow is the second primary color. Those with yellow in their auras are usually friendly and helpful to others. They are able to dispel fear and worry. Yellow stimulates the health and mental outlook, indicates an optimistic and intelligent individual who is very capable in business affairs. The brighter the yellow is the more intelligent the individual. Light shades of yellow can also indicate the development of spiritual qualities.

Green

Green is the color of healing and regeneration. These people are often individualists who show a high degree of independence. They are thoughtful and helpful to others. Green indicates energy, creativity, versatility, and adaptability.

Blue

Blue is the color of spirituality and inspiration. These individuals have much spiritual power to draw upon. They can have a harmonious nature and are self-reliant, confident, and sincere. It often shows artistic talents or dedication to a higher ideal. Indigo indicates a high degree of spirituality, integrity, sincerity, and wisdom.

Violet

Violet is rarely seen in the aura. It indicates the most evolved spiritual qualities, combining red (vitality and power) with blue (spirituality). It is the color of spiritual initiation and mastery. Violet can also be associated with power, influence, true greatness, worthiness, and altruistic love.

Gray

Gray is the color of convention and formality. Oftentimes, these people are loners but show powers of concentration and perseverance. A cloudy gray around particular areas of the body can also indicate poor health or depression.

Silver

Silver indicates a volatile, lively, and sometimes unreliable personality. Moods can change quickly. These people are versatile, active, and talkative. They may also be jacks of all trades and masters of none.

Brown

Brown often shows a capacity for organization, management, and perseverance. It is the color of the business person. It indicates convention, ambition, and power in the material world.

Although you may not see the colors of the aura immediately, there are other facets to watch for. The aura can be observed for its brightness and its width. Look for breaks or bulges in the energy, gray or black shading, or dullness. At first, the novelty of seeing the aura may be greater than your need to interpret it. In fact, the aura may appear to disappear just as you begin to see it. The explanation for this is that quite often your excitement about seeing the aura disrupts the experience itself, and your eyes fall back into their natural focus. However, when the novelty of seeing energy fields subsides, you won't have this problem.

You may want to experiment with different light sources and light levels for this exercise. A semidarkened room is often best to begin with. Some people have difficulty seeing the aura without fluorescent lights. It is also preferable to use a neutral color for a background to stand against. White, near white, or black are often the best colors. Again, with practice it won't make any difference to see the aura with only minimal preparation.

You can practice this exercise on your own as well as in groups. Use a mirror to observe your own aura, following the same steps outlined in the exercises. Or, on your own, practice during a meeting or lecture when you are feeling somewhat bored or daydreamy. Simply look at the individual who is speaking and relax, letting the aura appear to you. You will also find that you can practice with your pets. Again, the important thing is simply to practice.

"Life is like a ten speed bike—
Most of us have gears we never used."
Charlie Brown

How I See It
by
Lola Reppenhagen
Totally blind participant in Project Blind Awareness
(Reprinted with permission from Creative Community Inst., Inc.)

A year and a half ago I was contacted to see if I could get ten blind people from Buffalo to join ten persons from Niagara Falls to attend a pilot program on how to learn to detect color by feel. Needless to say, I was very skeptical. However, being a person with much curiosity and liking to be involved in everything and anything new and interesting, I said, "Yes, I would try." We went about seven weeks to this study and did something new each week. It was enough to intrigue us into doing more.

The results were so amazing that Carol Liaros decided to begin a new group and delve into this much more thoroughly. We began this about four months ago, and I find it difficult to believe the things that are happening. I have not yet learned to tell each color every time and some not as well as others, but it is coming. I have had some success with mind travel but not as much with mental telepathy.

Awareness of my own energy field is developing and I feel as though I can really see myself. I see my hands working; I see my body; I see images and shadows and seem to be able to almost see what is in a room. It seems that I really see it, although I don't and am totally blind.

Last Sunday I saw my first aura. A friend was talking with me when suddenly I saw her aura and was so surprised that I did not hear what she was saying. She noticed that I was not listening and said that my eyes got larger and larger. She thus knew that something was going on. I interrupted her and said, "I can see your aura." It was a white light, hazy and flickering that encircled her head.

On occasion I can pick out colors without thinking as I did recently when I "saw" my daughter in red slacks and white top.

Things are happening—I don't know why or how, but I do know that it would take a lot to make me stop this class of Carol's, and I hope she will continue to work with us. My skepticism is gone, and I know every day that something is coming from this experience to enlarge my awareness.

9 Blocks to Intuition
Tension
Perfectionism
Trying too hard
Intellectualizing
Terminology
Attitudes
Myths
Tension
Past negative experiences

9 Blockbusters
Relaxation
Concentration
Meditation
Playfulness
Receiving feedback
Changing the language
Not a test—a learning experience
You control it
Practice, Practice, Practice

The ideal conditions when attempting to see the aura:

- Comfortable room
- Soft lighting or semidark room
- White or black background
- Wear white or black clothing
- Use relaxation experience
- Half open eyes with an unblinking stare –a soft look
- Use peripheral vision
- Wear glasses? Try with glasses on and off
- **Relax** into the experience

EXERCISES

Seeing-the-Aura Exercise
(For individuals or groups of any size)

This exercise is important because it will facilitate your understanding that there is much more to "reality" than most people see. For example, this technique is used by a number of doctors, therapists, teachers (even parents!) for discerning how best to assist a patient, an individual, or a child. In time, it will also enable you to see the energy, dynamics, and thought processes that exist between people.

Exercise One

Prepare the room for seeing the aura. You will need a neutral–colored wall or screen. A projection screen also works well for this exercise. Next, get a partner or ask for one volunteer to stand in a position against the wall or screen, facing the entire group. (Or perform the exercise with yourself by facing a mirror.)

Sit comfortably with your feet flat on the floor and your hands in your lap. Very gently tell yourself to relax. Relax and concentrate, putting special attention on relaxing the muscles around the eyes . . .

When you're relaxed, here are several approaches or techniques you might try in order to see the aura:

First approach: Choose one spot on the wall several inches to the side or above the person's head. Then fix your eyes on that spot, without straining. Remember, relaxation is the key. Begin to relax as if you were at the movies waiting for the picture to begin. Working or straining won't make the show begin any sooner. Simply relax, waiting in anticipation, and it will appear for you. Without moving your eyes from that one spot, allow your attention to go to the area around the head and shoulders. Although your eyes are fixed on one place, you still have a normal field of vision available to you. You may have experienced something similar to this if you've ever watched someone out of the corner of your eye.

Second approach: Pick a spot on the person's head—the spot in the middle of the forehead is good—and fix your eyes on that spot. Now use your peripheral vision and let your attention go to the area around the head and shoulders, without moving your eyes from the spot you've chosen. Now, focus and refocus your eyes so that instead of looking at the individual, it's as if you were looking through the person.

For those who wear glasses, try these approaches with your glasses on and then off in order to see which works better for you.

Focus your attention on the area around the person's head and shoulders (or your own head if you are looking in a mirror) . . . Rather than straining to see the energy field, let the aura appear to you. Use your peripheral vision rather than looking directly at the aura. A soft, unfocused look is the best way to see it. Maintain a soft, unfocused look as you allow your attention to go to the area around the person's head and shoulders . . .

At first you may see a thin silver or white outline. It may appear as an intensification of the background color. This etheric double follows the contours of the body. You may also see colors radiating from the head and shoulders or from the whole body . . . The aura may appear as a pulsating, moving field composed of one or many colors . . .

Usually, the colors of the aura will not appear to you with the same intensity as the colors you are used to seeing. These colors are much more subtle, requiring a relaxed state of body and mind and a sensitive eye to see . . . The aura is not confined to any fixed shape but will shift and change as you watch it. It may even appear to be vibrating with bands of color which change hues and shimmer as you watch . . . Notice if there are any colors reflecting the health and emotional well-being of the individual . . . Ask yourself: "What am I seeing and where do I see it?" An individual's health problems (or past health conditions) can often be seen within his or her aura . . .

When you've finished, discuss your experiences with your partner or the entire group . . .

Ask for another volunteer and repeat the exercise. If possible, try seeing the energy fields of both a man and a woman for this exercise. Are there any differences between the two? Again, ask yourself questions like these: "What do I see and where do I see it?" "*Are* there any colors?" If so, "How do they appear?"

Make certain you take enough time to discuss your experiences with the group.

Exercise Two

Even an individual's thoughts have an effect upon his or her energy field. This exercise will let you begin to experience how someone's aura looks depending upon his or her current state of mind. This is a very helpful technique for discovering what is truly going on inside of a person's thought processes, enabling you to be of greater assistance to those around you.

Try the following variation to increase your sensitivity to the aura. Ask for a volunteer and look at this individual's aura as before. Instruct the volunteer to think of someone for whom he or she has negative feelings such as hate, anger, envy, or disappointment. Ask the volunteer to feel and experience that emotion. Allow a few moments for the experience.

Now look at the aura. Do you notice any change? What do you see and where do you see it? Discuss your experiences with the group and see how your experience compares with what the individual was thinking.

Next, instruct the volunteer to relax and think of someone for whom he or she has feelings of love and affection. Tell the individual to feel and experience this positive loving emotion. Do you notice any change in the aura? Discuss your experiences with the group, and then repeat this step with another volunteer.

Ask for a volunteer who has a headache or some other problem with the head, neck, or shoulder area. Have the volunteer stand in such a way that the affected area is visible to the group.

First look at the overall aura and notice its width, brightness, and colors. Then ask yourself these questions: "What does the aura look like around the affected area?" "*Are* there any differences in the color, brightness, or intensity of the aura?" "*Are* there any irregularities, breaks, or bulges around the affected areas?"

Now ask for one or several additional volunteers to send positive thoughts or healing energy toward the first individual . . . Notice what changes occur, if any, in his or her energy field . . .

Repeat all or any part of this exercise if time permits. Be sure to leave plenty of time to discuss your experiences. (Each of these exercises can also be done on your own while looking into a mirror.)

PROCESSING
Aura Seeing

Process what happened with this technique. What did you experience? What caught your attention?

What worked? What energized you? What were the low points? What frustrated you?

What has been your most significant learning? What are the implications of this learning?

What are some of the ways you could use this technique in your life?

VISUAL PERCEPTION OF ENERGY FIELDS

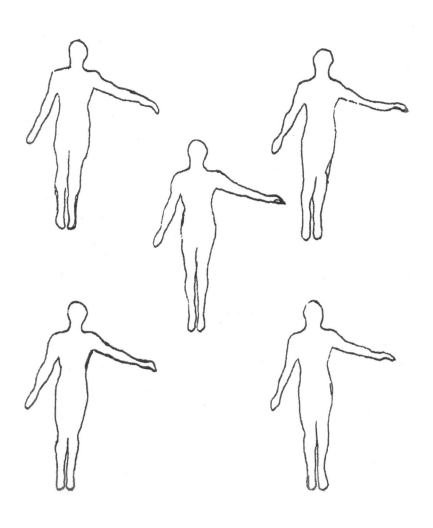

7

Psychometry:
The Connecting Link

I spent eight years as a research subject and instructor at the Human Dimensions Institute. Those years were some of the most important of my life in terms of learning to understand and discipline my intuitive abilities.

As a research subject, I participated in a number of different ESP experiments. Some of the most interesting involved psychometry also called "object reading." The experiments were conducted as follows: repeatedly, I would be handed an object enclosed in an envelope and told to report any impressions I had about the object. A research associate recorded my statements; this individual was also prevented from providing any feedback until after I had finished. When the reading was complete, the impressions were checked for accuracy. If any of my impressions involved precognition (the prediction of future events), they were kept on file and rechecked at regular intervals. Over a period of several years, this type of experiment was repeated hundreds of times.

Even now, one of these experiences is especially memorable. Just as usual, I was handed an envelope and told to report my impressions as I received them. I relaxed and felt myself connecting with the person whose object I held. I had a clairvoyant impression of a man wearing a suit and tie. Behind him were large burlap bags filled with money. From experience I knew that the man with the suit and tie was my symbol for a businessman, and I interpreted the bags of money to mean he was very wealthy. I reported this information to the research associate, who wrote down what I was saying.

Suddenly, I began feeling chest pains. It was a startling sensation. My breathing became difficult, and I had a sudden flash of pain that shot down through my left arm, obviously symptoms of a heart attack. At first, I thought I was the one having the heart attack, but it quickly occurred to me that what I was experiencing was the businessman's symptoms and not my own. This realization stopped the pain; and slowly, the sensations subsided and went away. However, I was still surprised by the suddenness and intensity of the experience.

"Has this man had a heart attack?" I asked. I should have known better than to ask questions during a controlled experiment because I received no response. The only way I was going to get any additional information was through my own psychic processes. I focused my thoughts on the prognosis for the businessman's health.

What I saw was unlike anything I had ever seen before, but it made sense to me nonetheless. I saw (clairvoyance) a horizontal bar, like a graph bar, which seemed to represent time for me. I knew (clairsentience) that the bar represented a period of six months. An image of the businessman appeared on the bar, and I watched as the image moved along until it came to about the midpoint. Then the image of the businessman disappeared. My interpretation from this was that he would be dead within three months.

I was asked to comment on whether or not the businessman should be told of his condition. I focused for only a moment before knowing that he had already made up his mind to die. Even if he was told of the seriousness of his health situation, he would not change a thing about his life. I stated each of my impressions.

After the experiment, I found out that the businessman for whom I was doing the reading was Chester Carlson, who was the inventor of the Xerox copying process and a millionaire several times over. He was a friend of the Director of the Human Dimension Institute and was financing the institute's psychical research program. About six months before my reading, Chester Carlson had suffered a heart attack. As seen during the psychometric experiment, two and a half months after the reading he suffered a second heart attack which killed him.

Scientists are actively studying the energy fields which surround the physical body. We know that the body, like any other physical matter, is composed of rapidly vibrating atoms and molecules, and this movement creates an energy field around us that extends beyond the body itself. This energy field is something like a fingerprint, and the objects we touch are also imprinted with our energy. We all have an energy frequency, and this frequency, like our fingerprint, is uniquely our own.

This technique for reading the energy of an object belonging to an individual is called psychometry. It is a simple process that enables you to attune to the frequency of another person's energy field by holding an object that belongs to that person. Used correctly, it is possible to receive impressions about an individual's physical, mental, and emotional health, as well as the person's past, present, and future activities.

This is the way I have come to understand the psychometric process: Holding an object belonging to another individual helps me to close a circuit of energy between us regardless of where that person might be. When this circuit of energy is closed, I am able to tune into and receive impressions about that individual. Whether the individual is in my physical presence or not does not make a difference to this connection.

When I was just beginning to develop psychometry, I heard so many different and conflicting stories about how it should be done that I finally decided to ignore the advice and simply concentrate on finding the process that worked best for me. In fact, those who tell you that the skill must be developed or used in a particular way are probably just telling you what works for them. It may not be the best technique for you. I found that the fewer rules I accepted, the freer I was to discover the techniques that worked best for me.

Some instructors put strict conditions on the type of object you could use or taught one specific technique for holding the object. I have heard a few "experts" say that the object should be made of metal, while others say it should be cotton or wool. From my own experience, I know of no limits on the type of object that can be used for psychometric readings. In fact, as I became more proficient with this technique, I learned that even a mental image held in another person's mind would suffice as an "object." It didn't need to be a physical object at all.

Some of the objects I have held for readings border on the bizarre: shoes, blood samples, photographs, hair samples, cassette tape record-ings (voice samples), eye glasses, various articles of clothing, rings, watches, combs, necklaces, handwriting samples—in fact, just about anything a person might own. As you can see, I found that the type of object is not really important. Any object can be used.

Some in this field will tell you that you should hold the object in a particular way for psychometry to work. It does *not* matter if you hold it in your right hand or left hand, in both hands, or place it up to your forehead (third eye). If the object is a chair, you might do your best work simply by sitting on it. The most important consideration is comfort. If it feels more natural or comfortable to hold it in one hand than the other, then do so. Find out what works for you.

Although there are no limitations to the type of objects that can be used, there is one consideration that should be followed: the object should be one that has been used only by the person you will be read-ing. This is to reduce the confusion that can result if you begin picking up impressions from another person who has handled the object. The best way to illustrate the confusion is with an example from my own experience:

One of my clients, a writer, had given me his wallet to hold for the reading. As soon as I touched it, I had the impression of a woman clutching her chest in pain and falling to a low table. The scene ended as quickly as it had begun. My client seemed surprised when I told him about it. The woman I saw was his wife. During a trip to Japan, she had suffered a heart attack and died, falling onto a low table just as I described it. But the strangest thing was that her death had occurred almost twenty years earlier! Although my client had carried the wallet for years, the first impressions I received were still of his wife who had used the wallet when she was alive. You can imagine the confusion, and the potential harm, that could have resulted if the wallet had been owned by someone completely unknown to the writer. The best way to avoid this confusion is to use objects that have not been in contact with anyone other than the person you are reading.

Many of the mistakes I have made in psychometry were caused by wrong interpretations. The impression was correct, but the meaning or interpretation I gave it turned out to be wrong. An example of this came during a reading for a woman client. I saw (clairvoyance) her standing beside a mountain. She began pushing and shoving it, but it would not give an inch. It was evident to me that the woman was not going to budge the mountain, but she was throwing most of her physical, mental, and emotional energy into the task. I was not sure what the mountain symbolized, but my logical interpretation was that it represented her job since that is the area of life where many people put their time and energy into. I told her that her job was taking all of her time and energy, and she did not seem to be getting any results for her efforts. She told me it was not her job that she was trying to change, rather it was her husband. They had recently separated, and she was trying to change his mind about their marriage. Her husband was the inflexible, immovable "mountain," not her occupation. The impression was accurate, but my interpretation was not.

Therefore, in the early stages of your intuitive development it is important to report only what you see, hear, or feel. The impressions you verbalize may make sense to the individual if they are correct while your own attempt at interpretation may turn out to be completely wrong. By giving and receiving feedback in the psychometry exercise, you will begin to learn your own personal symbols and check your own interpretations for accuracy.

One of my students told me an interesting story about one of his symbols. As a child, he had spent much time with his grandmother. She had cancer and was near death. One of his vivid memories of her was her habit of eating peaches and leaving them, half-eaten, lying around the house. As a result, his symbolic impression of cancer was a half-eaten peach. As he developed his psychometric skills whenever he saw half-eaten peaches, he knew that the symbol could be interpreted as cancer. Feedback he received from his partners told him he was accurate. Just as in this case, your impressions may be highly specific to your experience. Only by using your imagination and intellect and by testing your interpretations over and over again will you discover your own personal symbology.

There is another potential obstacle that can get in the way of accurate psychometric information. Confusion may occur when one receives telepathic information rather than psychometrics. For example, years ago I was often asked to predict the outcome of particular sporting events. Whenever "predicted," these predictions often turned out wrong. Afterwards, I discovered that these erroneous "predictions" often times stated back to the individual what the individual believed would occur. Since it is possible to confuse a telepathic message or impression for a valid psychic impression, only testing, practice, and accurate feedback will tell you if your impressions are telepathic or psychometric. In my own experience, I have discovered that if I receive an answer to a question before the question has been completely asked, it is telepathy, not an accurate intuitive insight.

The psychometric exercise that follows is a guided experience employing the intellect, the imagination, and the psychic processes. Many people believe you must somehow disengage the intellect before the psychic process can be engaged. This is impossible for most people. In this exercise, you will be using the intellect as a springboard into the imagination. Since the imagination stimulates the psychic processes, psychic impressions should be used in cooperation with the intellect and stimulated by the imagination.

This exercise is designed to keep the left brain (the intellect) occupied so that the right brain (the imaging part of the brain) and the psychic processes can be engaged. In this way, the intellect flows into the psychic. Automatically, the intellect collects visual and other sensory impressions such as body language, facial expressions, style of dress, etc., which in turn helps to stimulate the use of the imagination. What does the information you perceive lead you to imagine about your partner? Rather than forcing your imagination to work, let it operate in its own way and bring forth the thoughts, feelings, pictures, or experiences that it has for you. Let them come and go as they will. Later, when you share your impressions with your partner, communicate them as clearly and completely as you can without trying to interpret them.

The only instance of the intellect or the imagination creating a problem is when one or the other function is blocking the psychic process. For example, if the intellect is insistent on making only rational, logical deductions, then the psychic impressions will never have a chance to surface into conscious awareness. Also, if your intellect is discounting your experience with thoughts such as: "I'm not psychic" or "This can't happen" or "This won't work for me because I'm not good at this," the chances of success are very slim. Even if you are sure you are making the whole thing up, stay with the experience and put your intellectualizing on hold for the time being.

As you practice psychometry, you will notice that there are certain types of accurate information about your partner that you will receive more easily or quickly. The information you receive quite naturally tends to be in the area where you have the most interest. For example, if you are in the medical field, you may be most sensitive to physical conditions or health problems. If you are in the mental health field, you may be more sensitive or aware of mental/emotional conditions. Similarly, a banker or accountant may be more sensitive to financial situations or other material concerns.

The type of impressions you will receive and the way you receive the impressions may be uniquely your own. Some people are very accurate with names, places, and dates; others seem to be natural with personality evaluations or physical health diagnoses. Some professional psychics focus their work on finding missing persons or working with criminal cases—most often because those are areas of interest to them, so they feel quite naturally drawn to that type of work. The greater the interest in an area, the more likely is the chance of success. Even the types of impressions you receive may be related to your interests. A painter or visual artist may receive most of his impressions through clairvoyance, while a musician may be more attuned to clairaudient impressions. For the most part, the greater your interest in an area, the greater your chances of success. These early successes will pave the way for developing other skills later on.

EXERCISES
Psychometry Exercise
(For groups of two or more)

This exercise is a practical method of obtaining additional insights about another person. All of the following questions and similar types can be addressed through psychometry: "Will so and so fit into the rest of the team?" "How does my supervisor perceive me?" "What has my spouse desired lately?" "Is my child having problems at school?"

To avoid any confusion, participants should have a thorough grasp of the steps involved before the exercises actually begin. This is an important point and should not be overlooked. Read through the entire exercise before proceeding any further.

Choose a partner, preferably someone you do not know. If you're practicing with a group of friends, select as a partner someone you know the least about. Decide on who is partner A and who is partner B. Arrange your chairs so that you and your partner are seated facing each other about six to ten feet apart. Clear away any obstacles so nothing comes between you and your partner.

Each of you chooses an object that belongs to you, something that no one else has handled or worn. A ring, watch, article of clothing, eyeglasses, or even handwriting samples are just some examples.

For Partner A: When the time has come to begin, stand or walk over to your partner, and hand that individual your object. Then simply turn around and walk back toward your chair. Instead of sitting back down, however, you will remain standing, milling about and talking with the other Partner A until you are told to sit back down. (If there are only you and your partner in the room, pretend you are talking to someone, acting just as you normally would.)

For Partner B: As soon as your partner begins walking toward you, focus your conscious mind on your partner. When your partner hands the object to you, put it on the floor beneath your chair. For a few moments, watch your partner and notice as much as you can about this individual. Notice how your partner sits, stands, and moves. Observe this individual's facial expressions, the set of the shoulders, and the movement of the hands and arms.

Notice how your partner interacts with others. Does your partner do more speaking or listening? Watch the body language and listen to the tone and expression of the person's voice. This part of the exercise will help you become aware of your partner through all of your senses, and sensory information can be brought to a conscious level. This information provides a foundation, or a springboard, to the imagination and the psychic processes which follow.

Allow this process to occur for about five to ten minutes before switching roles. When everyone is ready, have the A partners sit down and the B partners walk over to the A partners to give them the objects. This will enable everyone to have had the opportunity to exchange objects as well as to observe their partners.

Take the time to become relaxed. Work with whatever relaxation exercise you choose to do. When you're ready, concentrate and place your keen, one-pointed attention into your hands.

Now you are ready to begin the psychometry exercise. Pick up your partner's object, holding it in any way that feels comfortable to you, and close your eyes. In your mind, imagine a duplicate of yourself standing next to you . . . and imagine your duplicate walking across the room toward your partner. If you are having a hard time visualizing this, "feel" that duplicate of yourself. In your imagination, turn around and sit down on your partner's lap, knowing that you have permission to do so. As you sit on your partner's lap, you begin to float down into your partner's body and you become aware that your duplicate and your partner have merged into one body. Become aware of this body. How does it feel to you?

Does your partner's body feel heavier or lighter than your own? Is it taller or shorter? If your partner is of the opposite sex, how does this body feel different from your own? What do these feelings tell you about your partner?

Now, as your partner, imagine yourself standing and walking around the room. You saw the way your partner moved, now experience it for yourself. This has nothing to do with psychic impressions, you're simply using the intellect as a springboard into the imagination. What does this tell you about your partner? Do you notice any aches or discomfort?

Now, as your partner, imagine walking out of this room and out of the building . . . Approach the vehicle your partner arrived in. What kind of vehicle is it? Is it a car, truck, van, or some other type of transportation? What color is the vehicle? As your partner, imagine getting into the vehicle. What position does your partner take: driver or passenger? Front seat or rear seat?

Because this is an imaginary experience, you are able to transcend space and time. Find yourself parked in front of a restaurant; leave your vehicle at the curb; enter the restaurant, and take a seat. As you seat yourself, you notice a waitress with a sour expression on her face approaching your table. She throws a menu on the table and walks away. What are your partner's inner and outer reactions to this person?

Your meal has been ordered, and as your partner, you are relaxing as you wait for it to arrive . . . Suddenly, you notice someone entering the restaurant. You are aware by your partner's physical, mental, and emotional reaction that your partner has a relationship problem with this person or has had a problem in the past. What does the person look like? What sex is this person? What is the person's age? How tall is this individual? What are the size and shape of his or her body? What is the color of the hair and eyes? What is this person wearing? Can you feel what the problem is between them?

From your own perspective, what do you feel would be a healing solution to this problem? . . .

Now that person turns and walks out of the restaurant, and another person enters . . . Because of your partner's very positive physical, mental, and emotional reactions, you know that your partner has great love and affection for this individual. What does the person look like? What gender is this person? What is his or her age? How tall is this individual, and what is the size and shape of his or her body? What is the color of the hair and eyes? What is this person wearing? What is their relationship?

Now that person turns and walks out of the restaurant, and your meal is served. You notice that there are some of your partner's favorite foods and beverages on the table. What foods are you seeing? What foods do you smell? You pick up the silverware and begin to eat. What flavors do you taste? Take a drink of the beverage. What beverage do you taste?

Now you have finished the meal. As your partner, you are sitting and relaxing, thinking about the activities of the past few weeks. What activities are you remembering?

As your partner, think about your plans for the next few months. What future plans are you making?

In your imagination, stand up, walk out of the restaurant toward your vehicle, and get in. Because this is an imaginary experience, you are able to transcend time and space. Once more, you find yourself in front of this building in which you are now seated . . . Get out of your vehicle, walk back into this room, and walk back to your partner's chair.

In your imagination, turn around and sit down on your partner's chair. As you sit down, you are aware of an interesting thing beginning to happen. You float up and out of your partner's body. Turn around and look at your partner. As you watch, your partner becomes transparent to you. You find that your attention is drawn to those portions of the body which are not functioning in perfect health. These parts of the body may appear brighter or darker, or you may find your attention is simply drawn to that particular area. What is the health problem? From your perspective, what could your partner do to correct this problem? Take time to note anything else you become aware of regarding your partner.

When you are finished, leave your partner's body and walk back toward your own. Next, turn around and sit down on your own lap, merging once again with your own body . . . Suddenly, you find that you are completely yourself again, totally detached from your partner . . . You are fully aware that all of your impressions were the work of your imagination, or so it seems . . . Now, open your eyes and become aware of your present surroundings. When you are ready, share all of your impressions with your partner.

One at a time, share your impressions with each other. Describe in detail everything that you experienced having the other person offer immediate feedback on the accuracy of each statement as it is shared. The sharing process is very important because without feedback from your partner, you will never know how accurate or inaccurate your impressions are. Communicate to your partner everything you saw, heard, felt, touched, and tasted in the exercise. Don't wait until your partner is through before responding and don't simply respond with a "Yes, that's very good" type of response. Instead, offer complete, immediate feedback.

Remember to give only your impressions, not your interpretations. Share one impression at a time, and be sure to give your partner enough time to respond. Be as accurate and complete as you can with everything you share. When one person has finished sharing his or her experience and receiving feedback, change roles and let the other person share his or her experience and have this partner provide feedback.

Psychometry Exercise
(For individuals)

These next two exercises are extremely helpful in assisting you to become more comfortable with any impressions you may receive regarding other individuals. For these exercises, simply be receptive to any impressions coming from an object and don't worry about having to evaluate what you are sensing until after the experience is over. Your friend, neighbor, or partner will give you the necessary feedback as to where you were right or wrong.

Exercise One

Ask a neighbor or a friend if you can borrow an object which once belonged to someone else (such as a deceased relative or friend). This friend or neighbor should be open to the exploration of your intuitive skills.

After working with your relaxation and concentration technique, take the borrowed object and focus on the objective of discovering more about the person to whom it once belonged. Focus your keen, one-pointed attention through your hands. Can you see the individual? What did this person do for a living? Is this a fun, lighthearted individual, or a more somber, serious character?

Allow yourself at least ten to fifteen minutes to imagine everything you can about this person. When you've finished, record your impressions. Return the object and get as much feedback as possible on your impressions.

Variations:

You can also try this experience with virtually anything you yourself come in contact with: an object you found, an antique, even a leaf from a tree. The only disadvantage of doing the exercise completely on your own is that you lack the ability to receive objective feedback about your impressions.

Exercise Two
(For this exercise, you will need the cooperation of a friend.)

Have a friend of yours gather eight to twelve items belonging to other individuals. Although these individuals can be friends or acquaintances, it's probably best for the friend you are working with to obtain objects from a variety of people you really don't know. These objects should be labeled with numbers or letters so that your friend can record your impressions and provide you with feedback at the end of the experience.

When the objects are placed before you, become relaxed and focus your attention into your hands. When you are ready, lift each object, one by one, with the objective of discovering to whom that object belongs. You might sense facial features . . . occupation . . . gender . . . You may see where this person lives or what members of his or her family look like. Whatever you receive, voice your impressions and have your friend write them down.

When you're finished, have your friend review each object with you and compare your description with what your friend knows about that person. See if you are better at tuning into certain kinds (or genders or ages) of people or certain types of objects . . .

"Imagination is more important than knowledge."
Albert Einstein

PROCESSING
Psychometry Technique

Process what happened with this technique. What did you experience? What caught your attention?	What worked? What energized you? What were the low points? What frustrated you?	What has been your most significant learning? What are the implications of this learning?	What are some of the ways you could use this technique in your life?

Problems with the Psychic Field

Many people of good will are repelled by the psychic field. Sometimes, perhaps often, people dealing in the psychic realm inaccurately name their work spiritual. Some of the problems encountered are:

Individuals set themselves up as gurus/teachers, expecting followers and obedience. Some of their behavior would not be tolerated in almost any other field, yet they attract people.

The names used by individuals: healers, psychic, medium, channeler, readers are foreign and often repugnant to many who consider themselves to be in the "mainstream."

The way work is done: the power is in the other, not in the seeker. For example, someone anoints you, makes you an initiate, passes on power, awakens you, cleanses your chakras, clears your energy, talks to a dead relative and tells what they said, heals you, etc. It is all very mysterious and the power in the situation is retained by the "one who knows."

Psychic impressions, voices, visions, feelings can be wrong—dead wrong. One right answer tends to create belief in everything a psychic says.

Psychic impressions are believed, even though the information or advice is poor. Some people seem to think that if it came from a discarnate spirit, the information has to be true. This is a serious mistake. Spirits are not all created equal. Some "information" gotten psychically is not worthy of attention at all.

People tend to give their power to those who can do mysterious things. It seems important to develop a healthy, yet respectful skepticism in the whole psychic arena.

PSI Metrics:
Tools for Measuring Psychic Impressions
by Ruby Gillion

Carol Ann Liaros, a Senior Trainer at the Edgar Cayce Institute of Intuitive Studies, has been a well-known psychic, lecturer, author, and teacher of intuition for decades. Ms. Liaros developed these techniques while she was a research subject for parapsychologists at the Human Dimensions Institute in Buffalo, New York.

During her eight years' affiliation with HDI, Ms. Liaros obtained 93–97% accuracy in predicting the future. She has agreed to share her creative intuitive techniques to help others use intuition in a practical way.

Henry Reed, PhD, a Senior Fellow at the Edgar Cayce Institute of Intuitive Studies, was aware that many of Ms. Liaros' methods shared in common a special property and that she had invented something of significance. Dr. Reed suggested the term "Psi Metrics" to describe these methods and asked me, a long-term student at the Institute and someone who has taken private lessons from Ms. Liaros, to write this article describing these methods.

What is Psi Metrics? By looking at the meaning of psi, a term often used in place of psychic, and metric, a standard of measurement, we have the meaning of a new term in the metaphysical field. Psi Metrics is a standard of measurement to be used for converting psychic information that may be nebulous into a form that is specific and more beneficial to the person seeking information.

Many different types of information can be obtained through the use of the Psi Metrics. These techniques can be used to determine the timing of an event, the location of physical problems, and to answer questions. They can help you decide if information is your imagination or an intuitive answer. If questions or statements are worded carefully, one or more of these techniques will provide immediate answers. The wording is of major importance in producing accurate results. These techniques are easy to use; and although they appear simplistic, they can be an invaluable aid in using intuition in your life.

"Mind is the Builder." (93-1)
Edgar Cayce

Psi Metrics Technique #1
Bar of Time—To Judge Timing of an Event

Jan	Feb	Mar	April	May	June	July	Aug	Sept	Oct	Nov	Dec

When a specific time for an event is needed, imagine a bar and label it as a bar of time. Divide this bar into segments designated as days, months, years, or any other time frame you choose. Place the event at the beginning of the bar and allow your intuition to guide the event along the bar until you feel/sense/see a change. You may "feel" a resistance that indicates this is the time. The "feeling" may be experienced in several ways: heavier, lighter, fuller, emptier, or you may feel as if it is stuck at one point and won't *continue* along your bar. Perhaps it will continue but will not stay; it keeps sliding back to a particular place/

time. As you allow your intuition to travel along the bar, you may "sense" that this is the place to stop. You may "see" the event vanish at a certain point, "see" a barricade that will not allow you to continue, or "see" a stop sign. However, you experience the difference; this is your signal for the time of the event.

Example:

Bob has been told that he is going to receive a promotion in his job. Of *course*, he is eager to know when this promotion can be expected. In his imagination Bob forms a bar of time. He decides to label the bar of time as 2013 and then divides it into twelve equal segments representing the twelve months of the year. Bob, while focusing on his question, "imagines" himself at the beginning of bar—January 2013. He very carefully allows his imagination to travel through the months paying close attention for any change. When Bob reaches September 2013, he experiences a difference in the way the bar feels. As he tries to continue to October, he finds he feels "stuck" in September and cannot move to October 2013. Bob concludes that his promotion will come in September 2013.

If Bob had continued along the bar until he reached the end and felt no change, he might decide to label the bar 2014 and proceed as he did for 2013.

Psi Metrics Technique #2
Calendar—To Determine What Month the Event Will Take Place

January	February	March	April	May	June
July	August	September	October	November	December

For some people it may be easier to picture a calendar with the months shown all at one time. Once you have formed the calendar in your mind's eye, hold the event in your mind with the intention of determining the month in which the event will occur. Then watch to see what happens. One month may light up, it may change in size, or it may flash. Once again, this is your intuition and the way you perceive the change is right for you.

Example:

Janice works for a company that requires advance notice for vacations which are scheduled on a first-request basis. She is planning to take a tour and is unsure which month would be best for her trip. Janice decided it would be easier for her to "see" a change in a calendar. She holds the question: "Which month would be better for my trip?" as she "views" the calendar. Janice knows that it usually takes a few minutes for her to "tune in" so she patiently waits for her answer. Her patience is rewarded as the month of April becomes larger. With this intuitive input, Janice can be sure she requests the best month for her vacation.

Psi Metrics Technique #3
YES/NO—Methods to Obtain a Yes or No Answer to a Question

Carefully word the question you want answered. Wording the question to be certain you are asking what you really want to know can be the most difficult step in this technique. Without precise wording, you may receive a wrong answer. Once your question has been worded to the best of your ability, hold that question in your mind and imagine/ see/sense the two words in front of you with the intent that the correct answer will come forward, flash, or change colors.

Example:

Ann has taken intuitive classes and is aware of the way she receives intuitive information. Now she has decided to put that training to use. She has been dating Sam for over a year and is beginning to wonder if the relationship is going to progress to marriage. Because Sam drinks more than she likes, she wonders if it would be good for her to marry him. As she prepares herself to receive the intuitive information she wants, Ann forms her question: "**Will** I marry Sam?" She visualizes YES /NO and almost immediately the YES begins to flash. Ann is pleased and sure that this is the right thing for her.

Did Ann ask the "right" question? Perhaps she would have been better served had the question been phrased as "**Should** I marry Sam?"

Ann may have received a different answer. Phrasing of the question can be of extreme importance.

Psi Metrics Technique #4
Traffic Light

Red = no
Yellow = caution
Green = yes

A second technique that is useful in obtaining a yes/no answer is the traffic light. As previously stated, be sure to word your question carefully. Concentrate on your question while visualizing a traffic light and "see" which color lights up.

Example:

Bert received a substantial inheritance from his uncle. He has five years before it is time to retire, and he would like to invest the money to supplement his retirement. He wonders if it would be better to invest in certificates of deposit, bonds, or stocks. The CDs have very low interest rates, bonds are good investments, but again a low interest, while the stock market is fluctuating but overall is in a decline. Still Bert has the potential to make more money for retirement in the stock market. Bert forms his question as "Should I invest in the stock market?" He then visualizes a traffic light and "sees" the yellow light is bright. Bert takes this to mean that he must proceed cautiously if he does invest in the stock market.

Psi Metrics Technique #5
Thermometer—A Method to Determine a Price

Sometimes a person has an item that he or she wishes to sell but doesn't know how much to ask for this item. Wanting to be fair but also wanting to get the best possible price, a thermometer can be used to determine the price. Also a person may want to buy an item and needs to know how much he or she should pay for that item.

The same technique can be used to determine the amount he or she should pay to purchase the object.

In your imagination, form a thermometer that is divided into segments representing dollars. You will have an idea of the maximum and minimum amount you wish to receive or to pay. Construct your thermometer putting the minimum amount at the bottom and the maximum amount at the top. Label each section of the thermometer with a dollar figure using equal amounts to ascend. Perhaps you will "see" a color move upward; you may "feel" it move upward until it stops; or you may just "know" when it has reached the highest possible point. At this point, you have your selling or your purchasing price.

Psi Metrics Technique #6
Etheric Form—Methods to Determine Answers by Asking the Person's Etheric Form

When you need information concerning another person, you can imagine the etheric form of the person. Ask him or her for the information you wish to obtain and watch to see the movement in the image to determine the answer.

Ask the person a question and watch if the person nods yes or no.

Example:

Linda has been having difficulty with a coworker in her office. The situation has reached a point where she must decide whether to look for another job or file a complaint with the office manager.

She decides to ask the etheric form of the office manager if something can be done to alleviate the difficulty. In her imagination, she pictures the office manager, poses her question, and watches as the office manager nods yes. By relying on her intuition, Linda feels comfortable knowing she will be heard, and the situation can be improved.

Example:

Ben has a restored car that he has decided to sell. Since he has restored the car spending much time and money, he wants to know the maximum dollar figure he can ask and still find a buyer. Ben decides to use the thermometer setting a base figure to cover only the price he paid for the car plus the cost of materials he used. He has not added any labor charges for his work in this figure. With this in mind, he establishes the base figure as $8,000 and that each segment would represent an increase of $1,000. Ben, knowing that he is a visual person, pictures the thermometer and watches as the color travels upward. When the color reaches $15,000, it stops and will not go any higher. Ben now has the figure he can reasonably expect for his restored car.

Example:

Janice has a new home and is looking for an antique oak bed for one of her rooms. She has attended auctions and estate sales looking for the perfect bed. She found just what she wanted at this estate auction, but many other people are also interested in the bed. Rather than get carried away in the actual bidding, she decided to use her intuition to determine what she should pay for the bed before the bidding started. If the bid goes higher than this amount, she will just have to keep looking. Knowing that she experiences intuition through her feelings, Janice formed a thermometer in her imagination. She experienced the imagined thermometer as being empty; and when she intuited the in-dividual levels, they "felt" full until she reached $1,250. Janice knew that she would bid up to $1,250, if necessary, but not go any higher.

Psi Metrics Technique #7
Do Kinesiology on the Person's Arm to Elicit an Answer to a Question.

Example:

Eric has been planning a fishing trip for several months. Steve was very eager to go with him, but Eric has not heard from Steve in a couple of weeks. He needs to know if Steve is still planning to go so he can make the necessary arrangements. Eric pictures Steve in his imagina-tion, asks him to hold out his arm so Steve can do kinesiology. Eric "sees" Steve hold out his arm and in his imagination tests Steve's arm to have a basis to judge the resistance. Eric hands him a note on which he asked: "Are you planning to go on the fishing trip?

He, then, tests the arm again and finds the resistance is very strong. Eric concludes from this that Steve is still planning to go on the trip.

Psi Metrics Technique #8
Have the Person Point to Area of the Physical Problem.

Example:

Megan has been fretful and has not wanted to eat. Karen, her mother, is concerned that something may be wrong, so she decides to use her intuition to find out before she calls for a doctor's appointment. In her imagination, she pictures Megan and asks if she hurts. Megan nods yes; Karen asks her to point to the part of her body that hurts, and Megan points to her stomach. With this feedback, Karen will make an appointment for Megan to be checked.

Psi Metrics Technique #9
Change the Image.

When you need to determine if an impression is psychic or your imagination, visualize the impression; then deliberately change that image. If the image changes back to the original picture, the impression is a psychic one. If the image stays the same after the change, it may be your imagination.

The Porters have put their home on the market and will be moving out of town. They have shown the house several times and have only one more appointment scheduled at this time. Mrs. Porter is very sure the people coming this afternoon will buy the house. Mr. Porter suggested they "test" her impression to see if it is psychic. Mrs. Porter visualizes her home; then, she deliberately changes that image and "sees" a SOLD sign over the house. To her dismay, she cannot "hold" the SOLD sign; the image of her house returns to the original one.

Example:

Jimmy has spent a lot of time practicing for the tennis tournament on Saturday. Because of the quality of the players, he decided he would be very happy to win third place; he feels he doesn't have a chance of placing first. Jimmy's mother suggests that he use his intuition to check out his placement by picturing the award ribbon for third place—a red ribbon, then changing it to the first place ribbon. Jimmy thought about her suggestion and decided to give it a try although he wasn't sure he had any intuition. Jimmy pictured the red ribbon, then changed the image to the one received by the first place winner. Next he waited to see what would happen. When the award ribbon for first place stayed, Jimmy was very excited. Even though he thought it was only his imagination, this outcome gave him more confidence in his ability. When the games were over on Saturday, Jimmy had placed first; his intuition had been correct.

Psi Metrics Technique #10
Where is the Problem?

You may feel uneasy but are not sure what is causing this uneasiness; you may have an irrational fear that you have not been able to change; or you may feel depressed but cannot determine what is causing this depression. It would be beneficial if you knew exactly where the problem originated: Is it emotional, mental, or physical? Could it be concern about your career, or might it come from a past life? The lives one has lived in the past can affect life in the present.

To determine exactly where the problem originates, picture a half circle divided into six parts: emotional, mental, physical, spirituality, past life, and career/job. Once you have carefully constructed your question, hold that question with the intent of establishing exactly where the problem began. At this point, "see" the five areas in the half circle and slowly go around the circle getting a "feel" for each one. One may "feel" different from the others; it may feel heavier or lighter; it may feel full or empty; or you may "see" one getting larger, brighter, or fade away entirely. The segment which "feels" different may be the origin of the problem.

Example:

Although everything in her life was going well, Teresa was depressed. She could not seem to find any pleasure in the activities that just months ago seemed so good. She dreaded going to the office each morning, disliked the idea of honoring the commitments she had made, and didn't want to talk to anyone. Teresa was afraid she was having an emotional breakdown but didn't know how to stop it. She remembered a program she had attended last year to help her learn to use her intuition. Maybe one of the techniques would help her find the source of her depression.

After finding her notes and the process that she thought would help, she constructed her question carefully and focusing on her question, she mentally moved from one section of the symbol to the other getting a feel for all of them. Then, still focusing with the intent to find the cause of her depression, she very slowly followed the segments until she came to the physical section. This section "felt" heavier—like she was weighted down. She moved on, and the heavier feeling left as she advanced to the past life section. Now that she had a place to start, she could begin the process of getting better. Her first step was to schedule an appointment for a complete physical in order to discover what had brought about the depression she was experiencing.

Example:

Jacob has been afraid of heights since he was a small child and had never been able to find the reason. No one had any knowledge of a fall or even a scare connected with heights. He was embarrassed by this fear as it caused problems when he needed to fly to another city for his work.

Jacob talked to a friend about his fear of heights, and she suggested he listen to his intuition. Well, he didn't have any intuition—or so he thought. His friend carefully explained about using the half circle divided into six segments: emotional, mental, physical, spirituality, past life, and career/job. He insisted he did not believe in past lives but agreed to leave that segment in as he was sure there was nothing to the whole thing anyway. To his surprise, as he focused on each area, one of the areas did light up. It got very bright! When Jacob realized that the past life segment had lit up, he was even more skeptical. He agreed to have a professional "do" a regression with him just to prove there was no validity to this "stuff."

During the regression, he found himself recalling a life in Hawaii. As a young boy, he loved the ocean and loved to dive from some of the bluffs high above the ocean. As he and some of his friends were playing on a very high bluff one day, this young Hawaiian boy decided to dive into the ocean far below. His friends were afraid and tried to talk him out of diving, but he knew he was good and could do it. A very strong breeze along this area of the island interfered with his diving, and he was swept back into the rocks at the base of the bluff and killed.

Jacob now knew the origin of his fear and could decide what he needed to do to get over this fear.

Psi Metrics Technique #11
In-depth Reading or Analysis

When you need or want more information about a person, the Twelve Areas of Attunement technique provides a model that can be used for focus. Beginning with number one representing self-image and self-esteem through number twelve which deals with the unconscious, institutions, and hospitals, the twelve areas of attunement are based on the astrology wheel and comprise all aspect of life. You may not need to go through each of the twelve, only those areas which are most important for your purpose. You may focus on each section in order or randomly choose the ones on which you wish to concentrate.

Example:

Garnet Charles is the Director of the Human Relations Department for a small manufacturing company. As the director for this company, it is her responsibility to hire all personnel. She has learned through keeping a record of those hired over the past five years to investigate potential employees carefully. She does a personal interview after the list of potential employees has been culled to five; and because of restrictions on what questions can and cannot be asked, Garnet has learned to listen to her intuition. When she began this portion of her job, Garnet realized that intuition would be very helpful and needed some technique to assist in getting the same type of information about each person. After working with several ways to gather the information, she decided to use a model of the astrology wheel which focuses on twelve areas of an individual's life. With this technique, she could focus her intent on all areas, if she believed all to be pertinent or she could focus on as few as one or two.

Her most recent hiring had been a young woman as a receptionist. This person needed to be pleasant, friendly, have good people and telephone skills, be articulate, and be able to use the computer to generate reports and letters. In going over the résumés of the five she was to interview, she soon found that there was not a lot of difference between the two best ones. The personal interview would be the deciding factor on the hire. Garnet realized that both these young women would be at their best during the interview, so she chose several areas of attunement with the intent to gather as much information as possible on each one.

Her areas of choice were:

1. What type of self-image and self-esteem does this person have?
2. What does this person value?
3. How does she communicate?
5. Is she creative?
6. How is her health? What is her attitude toward work?
7. Since this is a small company, how is she in one-to-one relationships?
10. What image would she project to our customers?

Before meeting with each of these women and with these areas for focus, Garnet did an in-depth analysis on each. After the interviews and with both sets of notes before her, she was able to choose the best person for her company.

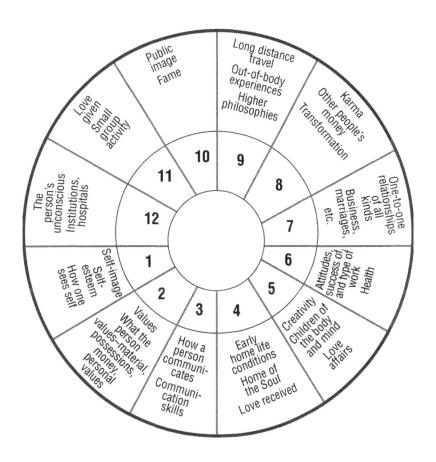

Twelve Areas of Attunement

9

Mind Traveling:
Exploration-at-a-Distance

Mind traveling is also known as remote viewing or traveling clairvoyance. I prefer mind traveling because it does not limit the experience to psychic sight. All of the psychic senses can be employed in this technique: clairvoyance, clairsentience, and clairaudience. This is an important distinction because for some people clairvoyant impressions play a minor role in their mind-traveling experience. You will learn through your own experience what forms your impressions take. I encourage you to experience and use as many psychic senses as you can, especially at the early stages of your development.

There is a distinction between mind traveling and astral projection, also known as an out-of-body experience (OOBE). Unfortunately, although these are completely different experiences, many people confuse them. Astral projection is an experience of being in two places at the same time. The term out-of-body experience describes this sensation quite accurately, because that is exactly what it feels like. I have had two spontaneous experiences, and in both I had a very clear, keen awareness of being in two places simultaneously. It was as though my conscious awareness had left my physical body behind.

During astral projection, some individuals report standing next to their bodies or watching their bodies from the ceiling. Others experience the distinctly uncomfortable sensation of leaving their bodies. Some experience a tightness or pressure in the solar plexus or navel area. Others have a sensation of rolling, swirling, or popping out of their bodies through the solar plexus, the heart, or the top of their heads.

Some claim that it is possible to induce astral travel at will, but I have never met anyone who admits it can actually be experienced on command. My experiences were spontaneous, and this seems to be the rule, not the exception. Some people I have talked to have reported more frequent spontaneous experiences as a result of their effort to induce astral projection, but for most it is an unplanned and spontaneous event.

The experience of leaving the body can be quite frightening, especially for the uninitiated. Some become so frightened by the experience that a temporary paralysis results. They may instinctively call out for help, only to realize that the tongue is paralyzed too. Many thought they were dying, and sometimes the fear of death will immediately snap them back into their bodies. Loud noises or other sudden disturbances can have the same effect, which can be an uncomfortable and even painful experience.

Astral projection is described here for the benefit of those who might confuse it with mind traveling. But, as I said, these are completely different experiences. During mind traveling, you will never have the experience of leaving your physical body or of being in two places at the same time. Whereas astral projection is an experience of leaving your body, mind traveling is an experience of stretching the mind or the imagination to encompass some distant place. Where astral projection seems to be a spontaneous and uncontrollable experience, mind traveling is a safe, controllable technique you can use any time you choose. I have never heard anyone express feelings of fear or discomfort from the experience of mind traveling.

In 1973 I initiated an intuitive training program for the blind called Project: Blind Awareness. This program proved to be useful to blind people of all ages, assisting them in becoming more capable, mobile, and self–reliant. Although the course consisted of many different experiences, one of the most popular and useful techniques we taught was called "mind traveling." A number of the blind participants became extremely adept at this exercise. In fact, one of the young girls was featured on *That's Incredible* as she was taken through an actual mind traveling experiment where she remained in New York State while her mind "traveled" to a target site in California. Cameras were at both locations recording the accuracy of her experience.

Perhaps one of my favorite stories about this exercise concerns a friend of mine from Buffalo, New York, who used the mind traveling technique she had mastered to help conquer a fear. Lola had been blind for over twenty-five years. At the time, she was planning to attend a conference in Washington, D.C. Because she usually traveled with her sighted husband, she was disappointed to find out his business schedule conflicted with the conference and that he would not be able to make the trip with her. She had been looking forward to the program for quite some time and was suddenly faced with an uncomfortable choice: she would either have to skip the conference altogether or she would have to travel to D.C. on her own.

For many blind people, traveling to unfamiliar places can be a very frightening and disorienting experience. Lola knew the only thing that stood in her way was her fear of traveling by herself. She reasoned that if she could only familiarize herself with the hotel where the conference was being held, she would feel comfortable enough to make the trip on her own. Therefore, weeks before the conference, Lola sat down in her living room, became very relaxed, and–using her imagination along with her keen, one-pointed awareness–made the trip to D.C. in her mind.

First, she visualized the hotel and its surroundings from a bird's-eye perspective, and then she projected herself into the hotel's lobby. Using her imagination and the power of her mind, she went through the lobby and took the elevator to the floor where her room was located. She noted the floor number and projected herself down the hallway to her room. On entering, she paid special attention to the layout, the placement of the furniture, even the colors of the room.

When she had completed her tour of the D.C. hotel, she projected herself out of the building, hovered over the hotel, and then brought her imagination back home. In her mind, the trip from Buffalo to Washington and back, a distance of several hundred miles, had taken only a few minutes. In that short time, however, she had gathered enough information and confidence to overcome her fear of traveling to the location.

Weeks later, Lola did go to the conference by herself, but an unusual thing happened when she got to the hotel. The desk clerk made a mistake and sent her and the bellboy to the wrong room. Lola realized this as soon as they entered, because the colors of the room were not right. One aspect of the Project: Blind Awareness program was to teach the blind to "see" colors, and Lola had mastered the technique. By sensing the layout and furnishings of the room, Lola further verified that there had been a mix-up of some kind. She told the bellboy that there had been a mistake because this was not her room. Humoring her claim, the bellboy checked with the front desk only to find out that the clerk had, in fact, made a mistake; Lola's room was on another floor. When she finally got there, she knew she was in the right place because the room was exactly as she had visualized it several weeks earlier.

The imaginary journey Lola took to Washington is an example of the usefulness of mind traveling, but it is not limited to the blind. It is a simple technique that anyone can learn and use. In fact, it is so easy to learn that nearly every beginning student has at least some success even on the first attempt.

Mind traveling is a technique that employs the imagination as well as the psychic senses. It is like taking an imaginary trip to a place you have never seen or visited before, and then making up a story about what you found there. The following short exercise will give you a brief experience with it:

Sit comfortably and tell yourself to relax. With your eyes closed, visualize the living room of your own home. In your imagination, visualize the shape of the living room as you generally see it. In your imagination, visualize the shape of the room and the placement of doors, windows, and furniture. Notice all of the colors and textures around you. Visualize as many of the details of the room as you can. Use all of your senses: Touch the couch . . . Listen for the sounds of the heating or air conditioning . . . See all the major pieces of furniture . . . Are you aware of any familiar smells?

Be very relaxed, letting the pictures come to you. Now, in your imagination, walk out of the living room and into the kitchen. In your mind's eye, visualize all the details of your kitchen. Use all of your senses: touch the objects on the counter top, smell and taste the food in the refrigerator, and listen for any sounds you hear . . .

When you are finished looking at these two rooms of your house, bring your mind or your imagination back to where you are sitting right now and open your eyes.

Using only your imagination and your memory, you can see how easy it is to "travel" to any room in your home. The only difference between this short exercise and mind traveling–and it is a remarkable difference–is that with mind traveling, you will be able to travel to a location you have never even seen before. You can learn to use the mind to sense whatever it is you will find there. With practice, you can travel to any unfamiliar location and be able to describe it, no matter how far away it might be.

As you practice mind traveling, you may be surprised by some of the impressions you receive. This is by no means an exact science. It is possible, even likely, to pick up confusing impressions that can only be sorted out by discussing them with your partner. I know of many cases where what appeared to be an incorrect impression turned out to be accurate in its own way.

For example, two women who were partners for the mind traveling exercise reported this mix-up that came to light as they shared their impressions. One of the women had received very clear impressions of her partner's home, and she was surprised when her partner told her the impressions were inaccurate. This woman lived in a small apartment, and the impressions described a large single-family house. As the two discussed it, however, they realized that, although the impressions in no way described this woman's current address, they did describe perfectly a home she and her husband had owned just before they were divorced. The question is why did this woman mind travel to her partner's old address?

The details of this mix-up are interesting and an explanation may help to explain some of the erratic or confusing impressions that sometimes arise. The house that had been described was the family home where she and her family had lived for twenty years. As this woman reported it, her husband came home one day and told her that he was in love with another woman and wanted a divorce. This took her by complete surprise; she had not been aware of any serious problems in their marriage. In time, however, she and her husband were divorced and she was forced to sell the house. She moved into a small inexpensive apartment which she disliked. All of her pleasant memories of home and family were wrapped up in the house she had sold. On an emotional level, she was still living there. Her heart was in that house. It is not too surprising, then, that her partner mind traveled to her "home" and saw the woman's former house and not the apartment.

Confusing impressions are not at all uncommon. If you have a confus-

ing image, quite frequently your partner will be able to provide information that will make sense out of the impression. For example, in the
guided mind–traveling exercise, I ask individuals if they see a fireplace in
their partner's home. In one of my classes, a man reported that he saw
a fireplace, a Franklin stove, in the corner of his partner's living room.
As soon as he made note of it, however, it disappeared. He decided that
there was not a fireplace there after all and immediately the Franklin
stove reappeared in his imagination. This went back and forth several
times, appearing and disappearing, until he was totally confused. When
he shared this confusing impression, his partner was able to clear up the
mystery immediately. He did have a Franklin stove that usually sat in the
corner of the living room, but he had recently moved it into the garage
because it was badly in need of repainting.

One individual had an unusual experience when she mind traveled to
the home of her partner who lived in the Buffalo area. As she was going
through the living room, she had the feeling that the room was too small,
and she was tempted to take out the wall between the living room and an
adjoining bedroom to make it more spacious. As it turned out, that was
exactly her partner's plan. He had already hired an architect to draw up
the remodeling plans, although the work on it had not yet begun. Like this
woman, you may find yourself traveling out of the present and into the
past or future. When this happens, there is often a very good reason.

These stories should help illustrate that confusing impressions may not
be inaccurate instead they may make perfect sense to your partner. If you
do receive confusing or contradictory impressions, be sure to communicate them as clearly as possible, without adding your own interpretations.
You will actually improve your accuracy by reporting your impressions
exactly as you get them, without trying to guess at their meaning.

Mind traveling has many practical uses. Visually handicapped people
have found it to be one of the most practical techniques of all. It is an
ideal way to acquaint them with unfamiliar surroundings, to decrease
their fear of new places, and to help them become mobile more quickly.
Mind traveling is one of many techniques that help them become more
capable, independent, and self-reliant.

Sighted people have also found some very practical applications. If
you have children, use this simple technique to check in on your children (or the babysitter) while you are away. When my own children were

younger, I would frequently mind travel to my home to check on them whenever I was out of town. On one occasion, I checked in on my teenage daughter, who was supposed to be home alone. During the mind-traveling experience, I realized that she was entertaining two boys in the living room. I phoned her immediately and told her to tell the boys to leave. She did not even ask me how I knew they were there. From my own experience, I can tell you that your children may not always appreciate your mind-traveling ability, but it can do wonders for a parent's peace of mind.

This technique is useful on the job too, no matter what your occupation. When you are away or on vacation, you won't have to use the telephone to check in at the office to see if someone needs you, you can mind travel there instead. You can prepare for meetings or sales calls at unfamiliar locations with this technique. If you are on a job hunt, you may become more comfortable by mind traveling to a prospective employer's office in order to familiarize yourself with the location even before the interview.

These are only a few examples of ways to use the mind–traveling technique. You can come up with several practical uses of your own. Make a list of the kinds of activities you are involved with on a regular basis, and you are sure to find some activities where mind traveling can be helpful to you.

Remember, you are more likely to do well if there is some motivation behind what you are trying to accomplish. There are many kinds of motivators: interest, curiosity, a need to know, a desire to help, and occupational interests are just a few. For example, an individual in one of my beginning ESP classes was extremely accurate in his description of his partner's home. He went into detail describing the room placement, the colors and textures of the furniture, carpeting, drapery, and many other details. As it turned out, he was an interior designer and his occupational interest had provided the motivation for him to do well.

Do not be discouraged if your accuracy is low to begin with. There is no one who is 100 % accurate with his or her impressions. A psychic-sensitive who is consistently accurate 80 to 90% of the time is considered doing very well. Approach your mistakes as opportunities to learn more and to continue developing your skills.

If you do find that your impressions are consistently inaccurate over

time, check your motivation. Is your practicing something that is important to you? Are you really interested in knowing the information you are
after? Are there any practical uses for knowing what you want to know?
If not, try other exercises or techniques that interest you more, or recon-
struct the exercise to more accurately reflect your own interests.

Most importantly, have fun with the exercise. A playful attitude will
not only help you relax physically and mentally but will also put you in
a good frame of mind for better results.

CHARACTERISTICS OF:

ASTRAL PROJECTION
OOBE (out-of-the-body experiences)
SOUL TRAVEL

▶ Distinct feeling of leaving your body and being in two places at the same time

▶ Usually a spontaneous experience

▶ May be accompanied by physical sensations:
   waves of energy from feet to head
   tightness in solar plexus
   floating
   paralysis
   buzzing; ringing

▶ See everything exactly as if you were there in your physical body

▶ Some authorities say there is a danger you may not be able to get back in your body

▶ Some report seeing a "silver cord"

▶ Sensation of "rolling out," "popping out," "swirling out" of the top of your head

▶ Appears it takes several years to develop this skill

MIND TRAVELING
REMOTE VIEWING
TRAVELING CLAIRVOYANCE

▶ No sensation of "going anywhere"

▶ "As if" the place comes to you—like remembering a place where you've never been

▶ No physical sensations

▶ Things appear hazy, foggy, not clear and distinct

▶ No dangers

▶ Can be "learned" quickly

EXERCISES

Mind-Traveling Exercise
(For individuals)

As cited in this chapter, the blind have found the mind-traveling exercise to be a valuable way to investigate an unfamiliar environment. It can also be extremely practical for such things as parents checking in on their children, business people seeing if they are needed in the office, or health care professionals checking in on their patients. This exercise, and the one which follows, will give you some of the experience you need in order to begin trusting your "imaginary" journeys.

This exercise will enable you to explore the mind–traveling technique on your own and then gather feedback to verify the accuracy of your own impressions. In this example, you will mind travel to a restaurant (within driving distance) that you've never visited before. Choose one from the yellow pages if nothing comes immediately to mind. Then copy down its address on a slip of paper. You may want to hold the address while you do the exercise.

To start, sit comfortably in your chair, close your eyes, and begin using your favorite relaxation technique . . .

When you're ready, in your imagination, visualize a duplicate of yourself standing next to you . . . If you are unable to visualize this duplicate, then feel this duplicate of yourself, or simply know that it is there . . . Label this duplicate of yourself, "your mind" . . .

In your imagination, project your mind away from yourself, out the door, and out of your home . . . In your imagination, project your mind up into the air and hover over the roof of your home . . . How do things appear from this perspective? . . .

Now, in your imagination, project your mind to the address of the restaurant and hover overhead . . . Take a good look around you, noticing whatever you can about the area where the restaurant is located . . .

Project your mind to the entrance of the restaurant . . . What does the entrance look like? Put your hand out and touch the front door . . . How does it feel? . . . What material is this? . . . Is the door solid or is there a window? . . .

Now, enter through the front door and look around you . . . What do you find to your left . . . to your right . . . straight ahead? . . . Does someone greet you at the front door? . . . If so, what does this person look like? . . .

Your host leads you into the dining room to your table . . . What direction are you going? . . . What table are you led to? . . . Be seated and pick up the menu . . . What foods do you see on the menu? . . . How reasonable are the prices? . . .

As your server approaches and greets you, notice the facial expression, the manner, and the tone of voice . . . How would you describe your server? . . .

After ordering your meal, the server leaves and you begin to notice your surroundings in detail . . . What do you see on your table? . . . Reach out and touch the items . . . What are you touching? . . . Is there a tablecloth on the table? . . . If so, how does it feel? . . . Run your hand over the table itself. What is it made out of? . . .

Notice the other patrons seated around you . . . Are there many people or only a few? . . . How are they dressed? . . . Listen to the conversation in the room . . . Is it quiet . . . noisy . . . boisterous . . . or low-keyed and serious? . . . Do these people seem to be enjoying their meals? . . . Do you hear background music? . . .

Look around you and notice the decor of this room . . . What colors do you see on the walls? . . . Are there paintings . . . wall hangings . . . or photographs on the walls? Do you see or feel any plants in the room? . . . If so, where are they? . . .

Now your server brings you a tray of food. On the tray are samples of foods this restaurant serves. What foods do you see on the tray? . . . What foods do you smell? . . . What can you taste? . . . Use all of your sensory input . . .

When you finish your meal, your server brings you the check. How much is it? . . . Is it cheap, reasonable, or expensive? . . . As you prepare to leave, take one last look around you and notice anything you may have missed before . . .

Now, project your mind to the entrance of the restaurant and out the front door. . . . Project your mind up into the air and hover over the restaurant . . . In your imagination, project your mind back over your home . . . And, then, return to the room where you are sitting . . . Let your mind stand next to your body . . . and now put your duplicate back into yourself . . . Begin breathing normally and relax . . . When you are ready, open your eyes, feeling completely normal, refreshed, and relaxed . . .

When you are finished, be sure to take the time to write down all of your impressions immediately. When you have time, visit the restaurant and check your list of impressions for their accuracy.

Variation:

You might try this same technique to visit numerous other places that you've never seen: for example, a new grocery store, an open house, a recreation center, a nearby park, or even a section of the library where you've never actually been (try choosing a book you'll like in your imagination).

Be sure to make note of your impressions beforehand and then follow-up with notes regarding what you actually encountered at the location.

Mind-Traveling Exercise
(For groups of any size)

The primary purpose of this experience is to obtain feedback from a mind-traveling exercise. However, you may also find it to be a valuable method of obtaining clairvoyant insights into your partner's life and experiences.

Choose a partner whose home you have never visited and sit comfortably, facing your partner. On a slip of paper, write your street address the way you would write it on an envelope and set it next to you. (Note: if you live in an apartment, DO NOT include your apartment number as this will be part of the experience.)

Become comfortable in your chair and relax. When you are relaxed, exchange address papers with your partner, each looking at the address. You do not need to memorize it because the subconscious mind doesn't forget anything. Then, sit comfortably with your eyes closed and relax . . .

In your imagination, visualize a duplicate of yourself standing next to you. If you have difficulty visualizing, feel that duplicate of yourself, or simply know that it is there . . . Label this duplicate of yourself "your mind." And then, in your imagination, project this duplicate of yourself, i.e. "your mind," across the room, out the door, and out of this building . . .

In your imagination, project your mind up into the air to hover over this building . . . Take a look at the building from this perspective. You've seen it from the ground, how does it look from here? . . .

Now, in your imagination, project your mind to your partner's address, and hover over this address . . .

As you hover overhead, look around you . . . Are you in a crowded and congested area, or in a quiet, open area? . . . Are you in the city . . . the country . . . or a suburban area? . . . Are there many buildings here or only a few? . . . Is this a business, industrial, or residential area? . . .

Now, direct your attention to your partner's dwelling . . . What kind of building is it? . . . Is it an apartment building . . . a house . . . mobile home . . . commercial property with an apartment, a condominium, or some other type of dwelling? . . .

Is there a garage? . . . Is it attached or unattached? . . . How many cars does it hold? . . .

While you are hovering over the address, pay close attention to all of your senses . . . What sounds are familiar in this neighborhood? . . . Is it noisy . . . quiet? . . . Do you hear any kind of commercial traffic? Are they cars . . . trucks . . . airplanes? . . . Do you hear children playing? . . . Do you hear water, like a river, a lake, a stream, or even a sprinkling system? . . .

What do you sense or feel about this area? . . . Pay attention to all of your sensory input . . .

Now, project your mind to the front door, and stand there for just a moment . . . In your imagination, reach out and touch the building's structure with your hand . . . Are you touching wood . . . siding . . . bricks . . . or cement block? What does it feel like? . . . Next, turn your attention to the front door itself . . . Reach out and touch the front door . . . What material is it made of? . . . Is the door solid or are there any windows? . . . Is there anything distinctive about this door? . . . Is there a number or a letter on the door? . . .

Since you know you have the permission of those who live here, enter the front door. Now, look to your left. What do you see, feel, or experience? . . . Next, turn straight ahead. What do you see, feel, or experience directly in front of you? . . . Finally, look to your right. What do you see, feel, or experience? . . .

As you stand inside the front door, your body begins to feel a gentle pulling sensation, and you find yourself drawn in the direction of the living room . . . In what direction are you moving? . . . Again, knowing you have the permission of those who live here, begin to explore the living room. In your imagination, walk around the room and be aware of its size and shape . . .

Put your hands out and feel the placement of the doors and windows . . . How many doors and windows are there in the living room? . . . Count the number of chairs in the room . . . If you notice a couch or sofa, what is its color and design? . . . Walk over to a couch or chair and run your hand over it . . . What material do you feel? . . . Is it cloth . . . leather . . . wood . . . vinyl? What texture are you feeling? . . . Is there a pattern or design in the material? . . .

Turn your attention to the rest of the living room . . . How is it decorated? . . . What color or colors are the walls? . . . Are there any paintings . . . photographs . . . or wall hangings? . . . Are there plants or flowers? . . . Is there anything unusual in the room that captures your attention? . . . Do you notice a fireplace? . . . If so, where is it and what does it look like? . . . Touch the fireplace . . . What is it made of? . . .

Take time to absorb the details of everything you've seen, and glance around the room to see if there is anything you've missed . . . What do you notice? . . .

Next, in your imagination, take a walk through the other rooms in your partner's home . . . Notice the placement of the rooms, their size, shape, and colors . . .

Let yourself be drawn to your partner's favorite room . . . What direction are you drawn to get there? . . . What room are you in? . . . Is it the bedroom . . . the den . . . the kitchen . . . the living room . . . the porch . . . or somewhere else? Why, in particular, is this place your partner's favorite? . . . Is it neat or messy? . . . Busy or quiet? . . . Is there anything distinctive or unusual about the room? . . .

Before leaving this room, you notice a book or a magazine on a table . . . As you pick it up, you are aware that this is about one of your partner's favorite subjects . . . Look through the book cover and read it if you can . . . Turn the pages of this book to see what is there . . . What is the book's subject? . . .

In your imagination, project your mind to the living area and take one final look around . . . Is there anyone else in the room? . . . If so, is this person male or female? . . . What is this person's age? . . . Is this person involved in some activity? . . . If so, what is it? . . . Are you aware of any pets? . . . Touch the pet if you can . . . What do you see and feel? . . .

Take one final look and notice anything in your partner's house that you may have missed . . . Do you hear anything? . . . Is there a familiar smell? . . . Now, project your mind back to the front door and leave the same way you entered . . . Project your mind up into the air and over the dwelling . . . Is there anything about the area that you may have missed earlier? . . . Pay attention to all of your senses and make a mental note of your impressions . . .

Finally, project your mind back to hover over this building . . . In your imagination, have your mind come back into this room, and put your mind next to your body . . . and now project your duplicate back into yourself . . . Begin breathing normally and relax . . . When you are ready, open your eyes, feeling completely normal, refreshed, and relaxed . . .

One at a time, share your impressions with your partner. Describe in detail everything that you received and experienced. Let your partner offer immediate feedback on the accuracy of each statement as it is shared. Don't wait until your partner is through to respond, or don't respond simply with a "Yes, that's right." Instead, offer complete and immediate feedback. If you saw something you can't describe in words, you may want to draw a picture or a diagram.

When one partner has finished sharing and receiving feedback, change roles and repeat.

PROCESSING
Mind Traveling

Process what happened with this technique. What did you experience? What caught your attention?

___

What worked? What energized you? What were the low points? What frustrated you?

___

What has been your most significant learning? What are the implications of this learning?

___

What are some of the ways you could use this technique in your life?

___

10

Healing as a Complement
to Traditional Medicine

Traveling around the country as much as I do, I have had the opportunity to speak to many groups that are involved with healing.
One thing I have noticed is the variety of labels these groups use for
their healing techniques: psychic healing, laying-on-of-hands healing, non-medical healing, paranormal healing, faith healing, magnetic
healing, and spiritual healing. All of these are terms used to describe
essentially the same process: the process of facilitating healing without
(or sometimes in conjunction with) modern medical techniques, surgery, or prescription medication.

Although I have always been a believer in the power of the mind
and body to heal, a family experience brought the reality of healing
even closer to home. My son, who was thirteen at the time, fell down
while he was playing and hurt his rib. I used a psychic diagnostic
technique to find out if he had broken a bone, and I saw very clearly
that he had not.

A few days later, however, he was still in pain. A visit to the doctor's
office turned up nothing. At that point, I tried psychic diagnosis again

to see if I could get additional information, but this time all I got was a blank wall. The mother in me had taken over, protecting me from knowing his condition. Because I felt as though I was being "prevented" from seeing his problem, I knew at that moment that there was something seriously wrong. Since I was not able to do the diagnosing myself, I called a friend who was a psychic and asked her if she could diagnose my son's problem. It took her only a few minutes. Finally, she told me he had cancer.

My husband and I took him to the hospital where the doctors ran blood tests, took x-rays, and then performed a biopsy. The tests confirmed what my friend had told me. He had a rapidly growing and inoperable form of cancer which had started in a rib, threatening his lungs and vital organs. I asked several doctors I knew, cancer specialists, to examine him because I wanted to be sure he had not been misdiagnosed. They all told me the same thing; he had six months to live, perhaps a year with chemotherapy. The prognosis was not positive—even chemotherapy would not save my son's life.

I asked the doctor's permission to take my son out of the hospital for the weekend and immediately called another friend of mine who was a healer. Of course, no one at the hospital knew my plans. *All* weekend my friend worked with him, giving healings every two hours for two days. By the end of the weekend, he was feeling much better. In fact, even my son was convinced that the cancer was gone.

The following Monday he was readmitted to the hospital and taken to surgery for a biopsy because the doctors were concerned that the cancer might have spread to the lung. To their astonishment, however, during the operation it was discovered that the tumor was gone! More biopsies were taken, and the results were still conclusive: there was no cancer.

I was very curious to know what the doctor had to say about my son's amazing healing. Twelve doctors, including one of the top cancer specialists in the state of New York had examined my son—all diagnosing cancer. The doctor I talked to seemed very uncomfortable.

"It was a misdiagnosis," he said.

I asked him how twelve doctors could all make the same mistake.

"Well, you know," he said, "medicine is not an exact science."

I thought, isn't that what they usually say about the field of intuition? Then I asked about the biopsies. They had shown conclusively that he had cancer.

He looked at the floor, and then he said, "We must have gotten all the cancer cells when we took the biopsy."

Medical people get a good laugh at this when I tell the story. I knew his healing was not the result of some kind of incredible biopsy nor was the diagnosis ever in error. When my son left the hospital for the weekend, he had cancer. When he returned a few days later, the cancer was gone.

Yet, in spite of that fact that many individuals can testify to the positive effects of spiritual or laying-on-of-hands healing, anytime I discuss the subject I can always count on someone to argue about its effectiveness. "It's all psychological" is a typical response. This argument goes something like this: some peoples' illnesses are more mental or emotional than physical. If they visit a healer, they go with the expectation that they will be healed, and so, in their minds they are healed. Somehow, this argument just does not make much sense to me. There are all kinds of sick people who go to their doctors expecting to be healed, and they often leave the doctor's office feeling as bad as they did when they went in. Some people refuse to believe in any non-traditional healing and so they call any unexplainable medical event "spontaneous remission." What they are really trying to say is that a condition went away and they do not know why. To me, this does not sound like a very persuasive argument against healing.

Today there is a growing body of scientific evidence that healers can actually change the properties of the body to promote healing. At one time, I had the good fortune to work with Dr. Justa Smith when she was beginning her healing research at the Human Dimensions Institute. At the time, Dr. Smith was a biochemist who was working with changes in enzyme activity. (Enzymes are complex proteins produced by cells in the body that act as catalysts for biochemical activity.)

In her research, Dr. Smith had found that magnetic fields increased enzyme activity. She decided to find out if healers could also activate enzymes by laying-on-of-hands. She called on Oskar Estebany, an internationally known healer, to hold a vial of damaged enzymes in his hands for a few minutes each day. The results showed that Estebany actually accelerated the activity of the damaged enzymes. Dr. Smith repeated this experiment with several healers, all with similar results. She concluded that the overall effects of the healer contribute to the improvement and maintenance of health.

Another scientist, Bernard Grad of McGill University in Montreal, conducted one set of experiments with damaged barley seeds and another with wounded mice. Estebany also participated in these experiments. Grad found that Estebany's healing accelerated the growth of the barley plants and the healing of the wounds in mice.

In other instances, Ambrose and Olga Worrall were often used as subjects for experiments on the effects of healing. In one well-known experiment, the Worralls accelerated the growth of rye grass seedlings hundreds of times faster than normal by long-distance healing; the Worralls were in Baltimore and the experiment was conducted in Atlanta, a distance of more than 600 miles!

Dolores Krieger, then professor of nursing at New York University, did studies on hemoglobin values in patients treated with a healing technique she called "therapeutic touch," a variation of the age-old laying-on-of-hands healing. Krieger compared hemoglobin values in patients treated by the therapeutic touch with other patients who were not treated and found that the hemoglobin values improved in those who had received treatments.

At this same time, some of the most interesting and far-reaching research was done by Dr. E. Douglas Dean, a chemist, engineer, and parapsychologist. A small portion of his research in the field of ESP was published in a book he coauthored, entitled *Executive ESP*. Always interested in healing, Dr. Dean decided to research the effect healers have upon the chemical properties of water. He decided to try some carefully controlled experiments, again using Estebany and other well-known healers, in which he would analyze the chemical properties of water after the healers had treated it. At first, he used ordinary tap water in the experiments. Healers held the vials of water, treated them, and then gave them to Dr. Dean for testing. After measuring and analyzing the water, he found the healers had actually changed the molecular structure of the water. The water was in a new, energized state, and neither freezing nor boiling the water would alter its new condition. The molecular structure remained permanently changed.

From these examples you can see it has been proven that healers can change the properties of the physical body by healing processes or techniques. Scientists are now discovering what healers have known all along: *healing works*. It is interesting to note that not all advanced nations have placed such a taboo on healers. For example, Great Britain has thousands of healers who work in hospitals side-by-side more traditional doctors and nurses. In the United States, more and more health care professionals are realizing the importance of having various healing modalities work together to help the patient. In fact, some members of the American medical establishment are already using these healing methods in their work.

I believe there are basically two kinds of healers. The differences between these two are important to know for anyone who wants to practice healing.

The first type of healers works by the giving of their own energy; they actually transfer the energy they generate themselves into the individual being healed. They may not be consciously aware that they are using their own energy, but the effects always look the same. After three or four healings, they look and feel exhausted. The more healings they do, the more drained they become.

You will be able to recognize these healers easily because they usually have a number of physical, mental, or emotional problems. I know one healer who has had a dozen operations; others seem to be constantly complaining about colds, flu, upset stomachs, migraines, and other problems. One of the explanations for sick healers is that they are taking on the illness of those they heal, but quite frequently this is just an excuse for the illness and not a valid explanation.

This erroneous attitude suggests that illness is the price one must pay for healing others. Unfortunately, the individuals receiving the healing are usually aware—at some level—that the healer is paying dearly for their health, and this can result in feelings of obligation directed toward the healer. I call this an emotional "hook," and it is an unhealthy situation for both the healer and the person being healed.

These healers often refuse any kind of payment for their work; in fact, many people share the feeling that healers should not charge for healing. It doesn't have to be a payment of money. Volunteering to run an errand, for example, is also a kind of payment, and it can help to emotionally free the individual from the healer.

It is interesting to watch the auras of healers who use their own energy for healing. What you see is a tremendous increase in energy around the throat area or what is referred to as the throat chakra (center). The energy begins to increase and spin, becoming very active and energized. When it reaches a high level of intensity, the energy is transferred through the hands to the individual being healed. The healer's aura, as a result, becomes smaller and depleted looking. The throat chakra is known as the source of personal will or what would be called "my will" as opposed to "Thy (God's) will." The healers may not even be conscious of this, but they are activating and using their own will and life energy, and transferring it to another. People can be healed in this way, but it takes a great toll on the healer's health.

Now let us look at another type of healer. In contrast to what I have just described, these healers seem to be abundantly healthy most of the time. If you watch their auras during a healing, you will notice what looks like an opening at the top of the head, known as the crown chakra, becoming wider as swirling energy enters through it. Rather than using their own life energy for healing, these healers are connecting to the universal source or God energy, and as a result, their auras will appear larger, brighter, and almost "sparkly."

They are usually aware of the source of their healing ability and the source of the energy. Some call it God; others call it cosmic consciousness, universal mind, or whatever name they are most comfortable with. This source flows into them, fills them, and radiates through them into others. Their healthy, energized condition is the result of an ever-abundant, never-ending supply of God's energy flowing through them. Those who receive healings from this type of healer do not feel an emotional "hook" as a result. In addition, because the pure energy is being funneled through the healer's crown chakra, the healer is receiving a healing at the same time he or she is giving the healing. When the healing is over, the healer will feel healthier and more energized than before.

Another important thing about working with healing is the fact that there is a responsibility which goes with healing. This responsibility concerns the individual's right to accept the healing energy or to refuse it. Every individual has free will in this regard. Healing energy can be used to accelerate health, or it can be used to assist in the process of death which in some cases is also a healing. The use of the energy once it has been channeled through the healer should be left to the subconscious mind of the individual being healed. A proper response for the healer is to let the energy flow without any stipulations on it. Rather than directing the energy to a specific part of the body, let it flow undirected so that the individual has free choice as to how it is used.

We must also accept the fact that some people do not want to be healed and despite everything they say about wanting to be well, may choose instead, subconsciously or consciously, to be sick. There are many reasons for this. Some individuals gain attention or sympathy by becoming ill; others collect on insurance policies through disabilities or want to be waited on, or cared for, or need the power that their illness can provide. Few people, though, are ready to admit that these are some of the reasons for their illnesses. However, as you work with your intuition, you will be able to tell. During a healing, you may experience this as a feeling of resistance to the healing. Whenever you feel a resistance, stop the healing and withdraw, because the person is telling you "I don't want this healing." On the other hand, if you feel an attraction or magnetism, even if the individual has not asked for a healing, that can be their permission to be healed.

The healing exercise which follows is a versatile technique that can be used by anyone at any time. Those who are in constant contact with people, especially doctors, nurses, therapists, or anyone in the helping professions, can use this technique to prevent "burn-out" from over exposure to disease. Use this technique whenever you are in a negative situation of any kind, or if you are feeling tired, depressed, or angry. This cleansing technique not only helps to transform the anger and hostility but also revitalizes your body.

One thing you will notice about this exercise is that it is devoid of any special rituals, movements, gestures, or statements. It is not the ritual of healing that produces the results; it is the level of attunement and the intent of both parties. Rituals can limit the opportunities we have for healing in our everyday lives. If you accept the reality that rituals are unnecessary, then healing becomes possible anywhere and anytime: at your desk, sitting behind the wheel of your car, at the sink washing dishes, or anywhere else you happen to be.

"The future of medicine is the
application of intuition."
Norman Shealy, M.D.

Healing Exercise
(For groups of any size)

The purpose of this exercise is to allow you to be a channel of healing energies toward another individual. This process does not take the place of medical healing, rather it can be used to enhance and facilitate the body's own natural healing mechanisms.

Choose a partner and decide between yourselves who will be the first to channel the healing energy and who will be the first to receive the healing.

Arrange the chairs in a circle, facing the center. You will need only half as many chairs as group members; for example, if there are twelve participants, arrange six chairs in a circle facing the center.

The individuals receiving the healing will be seated during the exercise; those who are giving the healing during the exercise will stand behind their partners. If necessary, however, the healing exercise can also be done with both partners seated, one sitting behind the other.

Now, take your positions. If you are seated, get comfortable and lay your hands on your lap with palms facing up in a receptive position. If you are standing, spread your feet slightly and put your hands at your sides.

Both you and your partner close your eyes and take slow, deep, even breaths . . . Gently tell yourself to relax . . . And relax even more . . .

For those of you who are seated: Become comfortable, keeping your feet flat on the floor and your hands on your lap. There is nothing mysterious about this, you are simply putting yourself in a relaxed, open, and receptive state of body and mind. Continue breathing slowly and deeply, relaxing and turning your attention inward . . . Maintain this relaxed, receptive state of body and mind throughout the rest of the experience while the remaining instructions are given to your partner who is channeling the healing energy . . .

For those of who are standing: Take a slow, deep, even breath and hold it to the count of three . . . Exhale slowly through the mouth and tell yourself to relax, knowing that the body follows the commands of the mind . . . Take another deep breath and continue to relax . . . In your imagination, visualize a funnel that begins at the top of your head and extends up into infinity. If you have difficulty visualizing it, feel it, experience it, or just know that it is there . . . Now, in your imagination, visualize or experience a purifying, cleansing, healing white light flowing down the funnel and into the top of your head . . . Visualize this pure white light filling the head and flowing down into the neck . . . into the chest . . . down your arms and legs . . . into your feet . . . and into every toe . . . While you are standing, experience yourself so filled with this cleansing, healing energy that it radiates from every pore of your body and streams from your hands . . .

In your imagination, visualize a small duplicate of yourself about the size of your thumb. Visualize this duplicate of yourself standing next to you . . . If you are unable to visualize it, simply know that it is there . . . Label this tiny duplicate your ego . . . and, with great love and compassion, project your ego into this tiny duplicate and move it aside for now . . . In your mind, or your imagination, set it out of the way . . . Continue imagining it out of the way until it happens . . . Your ego will find you again later.

When your ego is out of the way, place your hands on your partner's shoulders. Become aware of the energy flowing into you and through you, streaming out of your hands and into your partner's body . . . Don't direct the energy . . . Don't tell it where to go or how to heal . . . Let the energy flow where it will . . . Your partner's subconscious mind will know how to use it. Simply be a channel of healing energy . . . Let it flow through you, out of you, and into your partner in an abundant and never-ending stream of cleansing, purifying, healing energy . . . Take whatever time you need . . .

At some point in this healing exercise, you will become aware that your partner has received enough healing energy for this session. You will experience an inner signal that will let you know when it is time to stop . . . You may feel your hands become warmer and warmer as you channel the healing energy, becoming very hot, and then beginning to cool off. This may be your inner signal. Or you may feel a vibration during the healing which slows and seems to fade away. Or you may become aware of a sensation that feels as though your partner were pushing your hands away. Or you may simply know when to stop the channeling process. Be aware of your signal and you will know when to stop.

When you are aware of your inner signal, rake your hands from your partner's shoulders and put them down at your side. In your mind, take a moment to thank the universe for allowing you to be a channel of healing energy, and then visualize everything over your head returning to normal . . . Simply stand and wait (or you may sit if there are nearby chairs) until everyone has completed the exercise . . . (Pause until all are finished with their hands at their sides.)

When everyone has finished, continue with the following: Okay, now you and your partner share your experiences with one another. What happened when your partner placed his or her hands on your shoulders? Discuss what each of you was feeling during the healing exercise and where you were feeling it . . . Describe any impressions you received during the experience . . . How did the one channeling the healing energy know when to stop it? . . . Thoroughly discuss each of your experiences . . .

When you've finished, change positions with your partner and repeat the healing exercise.

Healing Exercise
(For individuals)

The following exercises all work with various approaches to exploring healing energy. These experiences will let you see firsthand how subtle healing energies can have a dramatic and measurable effect upon living things.

Exercise One

For this exercise you will need some dried beans or some flower or vegetable seeds, two small containers or planters, and some potting soil. Fill each of the containers with an identical amount of potting soil, and plant one to three beans or seeds in each of the containers.

Make certain that the seeds you plant (and the way you plant them) are identical for both containers. Mark one of the containers "A" and mark the other container "B."

Throughout the duration of this experiment you will identically water the containers once or twice a week as necessary. The only difference is that once or twice each day you will put your hands around container "A" for 5 to 10 minutes and send the seeds in that container healing energy. (You may wish to participate in a relaxation exercise before sending the healing energies.)

As the days progress, make a note of any differences between the seedlings in container A versus those in container B. Do the seedlings seem to grow faster? Do they appear healthier? Are there any measurable differences? Keep track of your findings.

Variation:

Follow the instructions for planting the seedlings as outlined above, however, rather than sending healing energies each day to the seeds in container A, instead "heal" the water you use to water the plants in container A. Every time you water, take two glasses filled with ordinary tap water and send healing energy to the one to be used for container A. Just pour the water into container B as you would normally.

As before, as the days progress, make note of any differences between the seedlings in each container. Does either of the seedlings seem to grow faster? Do they appear healthier? Are there any measurable differences? Keep track of your findings.

Exercise Two

The next time you have a cold, a cut, or any other minor physical problem, work with healing energies to help facilitate the body's return to normal well-being. In the case of a cut or a scratch, try sending healing energy each day to only half of the scratch. Does the skin appear to heal more swiftly in one area than another? Make note of your findings.

PROCESSING

Healing

Process what happened with this technique. What did you experience? What caught your attention?	What worked? What energized you? What were the low points? What frustrated you?	What has been your most significant learning? What are the implications of this learning?	What are some of the ways you could use this technique in your life?

Practical Uses for Intuition

DANGEROUS DOORWAYS TO THE UNCONSCIOUS

- Drugs
- Ouija® Board
- Séances
- Trance States
- Automatic Writing

SAFE DOORWAYS TO THE UNCONSCIOUS

- Prayer
- Meditation
- Intuition
- Imagery
- Dream Recording

SUGGESTIONS FOR NEW TRAVELERS

1. Don't be overly impressed with what people say they can do. Watch

what they do rather than listen to their words. Ever heard that advice before?

2. If you find yourself having unusual and exciting experiences, don't talk about them. People may not understand and may begin to wonder about you. There is a good deal of power dissipated by sharing personal experiences too early.

3. Stay within limits of your power. There are strong energies in the universe, and it is best not to venture too far out without an experienced, sensible, responsible guide. The psychic arena is not a game board; therefore, mistakes can be costly.

4. Test your motivations. Many people in the psychic field have strong control needs. New travelers are tempted by the power being discovered. Watch for pitfalls of the ego.

5. If you feel the desire to teach, avoid it as long as possible. A lot of harm can be done by the inexperienced, so give yourself time.

6. Try not to label yourself as anything exotic or esoteric. People are rightfully adverse to labels, and there is a lot of charlatanism in the world. There is a danger of being categorized with those you would otherwise avoid.

7. Try to keep explanations simple and concrete. Avoid esoteric language as much as possible, because no one likes to be left out with jargon language. If you want people to take you seriously, avoid unusual behavior and unfamiliar jargon.

8. There is a difference between people who are spiritual and those who are psychic. One way of making a determination is to check on how simple, normal, and respectful a person is. If the person is willing to "chop wood and carry water" with the rest of humanity, that is a good sign. If the person uses no labels and draws no special attention to himself or herself, you may have found a truly high teacher. The more wise, loving, and forgiving a person is, the more likely he or she could be in the spiritual category.

PRACTICAL USES FOR INTUITION

The ways in which intuitive insights can be made practical in daily life are innumerable. Individuals taking my workshops are always able to suggest practical uses or interests. It is important to keep in mind that psychic information is used most effectively when it is simply another component in any list of ingredients which combine together for decision-making, for brainstorming, for planning, or for whatever activity with which you are currently involved.

Airline Pilot

- assess crew better and faster
- assess the most important information to solve a problem faster and more accurately
- assess whether a particular passenger, once airborne, will give the crew problems
- precognition of any dangers (weather, turbulence, mechanical problems, etc.)

Attorney

- evaluate credibility of witness/discover when someone is lying or telling the truth
- scan statements, contracts, reports, etc. for distillation of important information
- determine which evidence will prove most effective
- scan lists of previous opinions by judges, arbitrators, etc. which might have bearing or impact or present situation

Business Consultant

- scan a management personnel listing for potential individuals and talented personnel
- evaluate realities of companies' present financial situation
- scan business listings as well as current, potential, and should-be-avoided clients to discover what clients are really thinking about the consulting measures being suggested

Insurance Agent

- assess what needs to be documented
- determine when something doesn't feel "right"

- foresee opportunities and dangers
- scan for best clients

Management Professional

- evaluate and set directions, goals, and visions
- discover how each member of a group or team can best contribute
- discover what will best energize and motivate participants
- scan for untapped talented personnel
- evaluate the main challenges faced by the group
- assist in distribution of delegated functions to staff

Parent

- assess child's health and well-being
- check in on child at home or school
- evaluate all sides of family disagreements or arguments with friends
- precognition of any potential dangers
- help to facilitate the child's natural healing processes
- help hyperactive child learn to relax

Personnel Manager

- scan résumés for potential hires
- evaluate which personnel need what training
- discover the root of employee problems/difficulties
- evaluate ways to encourage, boost morale, and facilitate a team environment

Physician/Nurse/Health Care Practitioner

- scan patient for overall assessment
- supplement medical care with healing
- evaluate medical techniques for those which are most effective for individual patient
- teach patients relaxation and stress reduction

Real Estate Investor

- scan properties for those which are best to buy, rent, or sell
- mind travel to various properties for preliminary assessment
- scan real estate agents for best sales agent and advertising vehicles
- scan property to determine where structural problems exist
- evaluate financing possibilities before undertaking loan

Stock Investor

- evaluate market trends and forecasts
- scan stocks to decide which are best to buy or sell
- discover the internal dynamics/problems/possibilities of a particular business

Student

- scan newspapers to find appropriate part-time job
- evaluate which classes are most suitable to your needs or skills
- scan books for required reference information
- assess potential relationships and friendships

Teachers

- assess teaching plan for student or class reaction
- scan student names for special needs, talents, and problems
- discover the root of student difficulties at home and school
- evaluate ways to boost enthusiasm in classroom

Vice-President of Sales

- evaluate clients (who will buy, who is considering another company, who is a dead-end, etc.)
- scan résumé and evaluate potential sales reps
- scan for potential new customers
- match sales reps with clients based on mutual affinity
- evaluate what is coming up in business life of major clients

Volunteer for AIDS Patients

- find best lawyer for clients
- evaluate potential medical strategies
- find best health care provided, doctor, hospice
- work with healing energies

Workshop Facilitator Organizer

- scan list of advertising vehicles to determine which will draw the most participants
- scan potential speakers for the one most suitable for a planned program
- assess program schedule for participant reaction
- mind travel to possible host facilities for preliminary site visit

Conclusion

The practical use of intuition should be a normal, safe approach to utilizing information and insights that are available to every one of us. Psychic ability is not something extraordinary, or unsafe, or evil, nor is it something "special" that is available to only a few. By itself, it is not necessarily good or bad; like many things, it depends upon the use to which it is put. The best use of psychic information, as with any talent, is to provide assistance to someone in need. Your use of ESP should be for the highest good of a group for healing purposes, for reconciliation, for love, for forgiveness, for problem solving, etc.

There are many ways to develop your intuitive abilities. The exercises offered in this book are techniques I have used in workshops and training programs that have proven most effective for people. Everything contained in *Unlocking Your Intuition* is designed to be safe, manageable, and controllable—experiences allowing all people who desire it the opportunity to develop their own intuitive potential. However, there are several things that should be kept in mind as you continue to explore the realms of intuition:

First of all, just as some people think psychic ability is something available to only a few, others believe that the information itself is "special" or should somehow be given more credence than other kinds of information. This is simply not the case. Valid psychic impressions and feelings can be wrong. In other words, just because something is psychic does not mean it is always the advice that you might receive from a trusted friend. If the advice is good, you may wish to consider following it; if bad, perhaps the information should be left alone. All psychic insights should be evaluated and given appropriate feedback based upon everything else that is known about a situation.

Secondly, without the proper background and precautions, there can be dangers associated with the process of entering into altered states of consciousness. Although the exercises in this book are safe, not all psychic experiences are. There are certain areas of psychic involvement that can be dangerous and should be avoided. Stay away from such things as automatic writing, games such as the Ouija® board, séances, and mind–altering drugs. These things can open up individuals to other levels of awareness for which they are unprepared. Mediumship can also be very dangerous, especially in the hands of unskilled or unprofessional mediums. It is also important to remember that just because a person has a certain degree of psychic development does not mean that that individual is spiritual. As in any field of endeavor, people are people and need to be evaluated on who they are, not on what they can do.

As you progress on the path of psychic and spiritual development, you should also take steps to protect yourself from undesirable influences. Raising the frequency of the aura creates an energy pattern that is finer, brighter, and more intense. As a result, you are more susceptible to the lower, denser vibrations of others who are attracted to you because of your positive energy. For this reason, mystics and psychics through the ages have cautioned students on the dangers of psychic development without any accompanying interest in personal, ethical, and spiritual development.

As you become more sensitive to the frequencies of energy fields, you will want to keep your own energy pattern in the most positive frequency at all times, thereby forming a protection of higher frequency around you. The emotions of fear, anger, jealousy, envy, hate, greed, and base desires all create negative frequencies. However, these dense, slow vibrations cannot connect with higher, finer vibrations. Even though you may become more sensitive to the moods, fears, and problems of others, these frequencies cannot affect your own as long as your maintain a positive, objective orientation. You can protect yourself from lower frequencies by practicing cleansing techniques or spiritual meditations. The object of this practice is to develop a continuity of consciousness so that at no time do you surrender your will to another person or to an unknown source. By doing so, negative vibrations around you can become transformed.

The healing exercise is both a healing and cleansing technique that you can use at any time to raise your rate of vibration and to protect you from outside influences. I know of no technique that will change negativeness to positiveness faster, or more effectively, than this one. This cleansing technique, which can be used to cleanse and protect yourself and others, should be used before meditation and every psychic exercise you practice. Use it whenever you find yourself feeling any negative vibration: fear, anger, depression, etc., or whenever you feel negative vibrations from another person, place, or unknown source. It is also a good idea to use cleansing techniques or prayer at the beginning and end of each day.

I often get questions from individuals concerning the right and wrong use of psychic abilities. Certainly, good common sense is always your most valuable guide, but most often I hear this: never go to any place you have not been invited. Psychic discernment is as important as any valid intuitive insight.

As you continue to work with your intuition, you will discover that some psychic techniques will appeal more than others. Although you may find that you are more naturally adept at one technique than you are at another, remember it is to your benefit to develop all of your psychic senses. And continue to have fun while you're exploring your intuition in this process of self-discovery and personal unfolding.

I hope that each of your experiences with *Unlocking Your Intuition* is enriching, uplifting, and positive.

Carol Ann Liaros
PO Box 745
Amherst, NY 14226
www.carolannliaros.com
caliaros@msn.com
(716) 876-4414

4TH DIMENSION PRESS

An Imprint of A.R.E. Press

4th Dimension Press is an imprint of A.R.E. Press, the publishing division of Edgar Cayce's Association for Research and Enlightenment (A.R.E.).

We publish books, DVDs, and CDs in the fields of intuition, psychic abilities, ancient mysteries, philosophy, comparative religious studies, personal and spiritual development, and holistic health.

For more information, or to receive a catalog, contact us by mail, phone, or online at:

4th Dimension Press
215 67th Street
Virginia Beach, VA 23451-2061
800-333-4499

4THDIMENSIONPRESS.COM

Who Was Edgar Cayce?
Twentieth Century Psychic and Medical Clairvoyant

Edgar Cayce (pronounced Kay-Cee, 1877-1945) has been called the "sleeping prophet," the "father of holistic medicine," and the most-documented psychic of the 20th century. For more than 40 years of his adult life, Cayce gave psychic "readings" to thousands of seekers while in an unconscious state, diagnosing illnesses and revealing lives lived in the past and prophecies yet to come. But who, exactly, was Edgar Cayce?

Cayce was born on a farm in Hopkinsville, Kentucky, in 1877, and his psychic abilities began to appear as early as his childhood. He was able to see and talk to his late grandfather's spirit, and often played with "imaginary friends" whom he said were spirits on the other side. He also displayed an uncanny ability to memorize the pages of a book simply by sleeping on it. These gifts labeled the young Cayce as strange, but all Cayce really wanted was to help others, especially children.

Later in life, Cayce would find that he had the ability to put himself into a sleep-like state by lying down on a couch, closing his eyes, and folding his hands over his stomach. In this state of relaxation and meditation, he was able to place his mind in contact with all time and space—the universal consciousness, also known as the super-conscious mind. From there, he could respond to questions as broad as, "What are the secrets of the universe?" and "What is my purpose in life?" to as specific as, "What can I do to help my arthritis?" and "How were the pyramids of Egypt built?" His responses to these questions came to be called "readings," and their insights offer practical help and advice to individuals even today.

The majority of Edgar Cayce's readings deal with holistic health and the treatment of illness. Yet, although best known for this material, the sleeping Cayce did not seem to be limited to concerns about the physical body. In fact, in their entirety, the readings discuss an astonishing 10,000 different topics. This vast array of subject matter can be narrowed down into a smaller group of topics that, when compiled together, deal with the following five categories: (1) Health-Related Information; (2) Philosophy and Reincarnation; (3) Dreams and Dream Interpretation; (4) ESP and Psychic Phenomena; and (5) Spiritual Growth, Meditation, and Prayer.

Learn more at EdgarCayce.org.

What Is A.R.E.?

Edgar Cayce founded the non-profit Association for Research and Enlightenment (A.R.E.) in 1931, to explore spirituality, holistic health, intuition, dream interpretation, psychic development, reincarnation, and ancient mysteries—all subjects that frequently came up in the more than 14,000 documented psychic readings given by Cayce.

The Mission of the A.R.E. is to help people transform their lives for the better, through research, education, and application of core concepts found in the Edgar Cayce readings and kindred materials that seek to manifest the love of God and all people and promote the purposefulness of life, the oneness of God, the spiritual nature of humankind, and the connection of body, mind, and spirit.

With an international headquarters in Virginia Beach, Va., a regional headquarters in Houston, regional representatives throughout the U.S., Edgar Cayce Centers in more than thirty countries, and individual members in more than seventy countries, the A.R.E. community is a global network of individuals.

A.R.E. conferences, international tours, camps for children and adults, regional activities, and study groups allow like-minded people to gather for educational and fellowship opportunities worldwide.

A.R.E. offers membership benefits and services that include a quarterly body-mind-spirit member magazine, Venture Inward, a member newsletter covering the major topics of the readings, and access to the entire set of readings in an exclusive online database.

Learn more at EdgarCayce.org.

EDGARCAYCE.ORG